U0558856

The MACAT Library
世界思想宝库钥匙丛书

解析马克斯·韦伯

《新教伦理与资本主义精神》

AN ANALYSIS OF

MAX WEBER'S

THE PROTESTANT ETHIC AND THE SPIRIT OF CAPITALISM

Sebastián G. Guzmán　James Hill ◎ 著

杨静 ◎ 译

 上海外语教育出版社
外教社 SHANGHAI FOREIGN LANGUAGE EDUCATION PRESS

 MACAT

目　录

CONTENTS

引言

要 点

- 马克斯·韦伯 1864 年出生于普鲁士*，是社会学*（社会历史和功能研究）的先驱人物之一；他在患神经衰弱之后写出了《新教伦理与资本主义精神》。

- 《新教伦理与资本主义精神》提出，宗教观念有助于解释社会如何形成不同的经济和社会结构。

- 《新教伦理与资本主义精神》是 20 世纪社会学经典名著之一。

马克斯·韦伯其人

《新教伦理与资本主义精神》的作者马克斯·韦伯是现代社会学的奠基人之一，也是 20 世纪最重要的思想家之一。1864 年，韦伯出生于爱尔福特市，靠近现代德国的中心。他的专业是法律，博士论文和"教授资格"*论文（即博士后）研究的都是经济和法律的历史问题。30 岁时，韦伯成为弗赖堡大学*的经济学教授，两年后他到海德堡大学*任教。

1897 年，韦伯因患上严重的神经衰弱而被迫停止教学到 1902 年，1903 年到 1919 年再度复发。患病五年后，韦伯恢复良好并写出了《新教伦理与资本主义精神》。这对他个人的意义十分重大，因为他强烈地认同自己所描述的孤独、自立的清教徒*具有禁欲*——忘我——的性格。清教徒是现代基督教新教*一个教派*的信徒，他们要在基督教信仰中清除罗马天主教*的影响。用韦伯妻子的话来说，这项研究"再次照亮了韦伯的心"，并让他"找到了自我"。[1]

韦伯从 1898 年开始着手研究，1903 年至 1905 年间写出了《新教伦理与资本主义精神》，并于 1904 年和 1905 年分两次发表在《社会科学与社会政治学文献》*上。1919 年，韦伯对论文进行了修改，增加了扩展的脚注，以回应批评者的观点，最终定稿于 1920 年并出版成书。《新教伦理与资本主义精神》一书使韦伯成为 20 世纪最重要的思想家之一。

《新教伦理与资本主义精神》的主要内容

韦伯提出了新教信仰与资本主义*（这是今天在西方占主导地位的社会和经济体系，私人掌握着贸易和工业并从中获利）是否存在必然联系的问题。这个重要的问题挑战了当时流行的一些观点，他们认为资本主义社会的特征来自既存的经济条件或物质利益，而韦伯认为观念也很重要，而观念不受经济利益的制约。他认为，我们无法仅从物质或经济利益中找到一种"资本主义精神"*的存在，因为这种精神似乎只存在于特定时期特定地区的特定团体中，因此必须考察其他原因。

在韦伯看来，"资本主义精神"必须与特定人群所持有的信仰类型联系起来。他认为这种信仰类型很可能就是宗教信仰，由于罗马天主教徒和新教徒的职业道德有着明显的差异。韦伯认为，罗马天主教徒不像新教徒那样乐于投身商业或其他专门行业，他们通常也不如新教徒富裕。他认为，这种差异是由于罗马天主教徒的宗教文化取向造成的，这种文化取向使他们不如他们的新教徒邻居那样会做生意。

韦伯还指出，西欧和美国的资本主义不同于世界其他地方所实行的资本主义。西方资本主义具有某些特性：它以合理的、有计划的方式组织自由劳动，并系统地追求利润。韦伯认为，要理解资本主义的起源，我们应该探究指导它的"精神"的起源。由于这种精神似乎普遍存在于新教徒中，韦伯想要探寻宗教信仰是否对资本主义存在影响，以及如何影响。

韦伯认为，一些新教教派鼓励禁欲苦行般的工作——工作不是为了获得愉悦，而是为了追求利润。比如马丁·路德＊（16世纪基督教新教的重要创始人）提出的天职观＊、加尔文宗＊的预定论＊。"加尔文主义"是新教的一个分支，对某些基督教教义持有特定的解释，其"预定论"是指上帝已经预先决定了一切，特别是谁能上天堂的问题。

在以上两个教派中，个人都将工作视为表明他们被上帝"拣选"的方式。韦伯认为，这种伦理也已成为世俗＊（即非宗教的）伦理了。这种世俗化的新教伦理促成了自18世纪以来西方资本主义的兴起，那时预定论和禁欲工作的美德开始流行。

《新教伦理与资本主义精神》自出版之日起，就赢得了社会学家的广泛赞誉，同时也招致了一大片批评之声。那些对现代资本主义兴起持异议的反对者们，围绕"韦伯命题"展开了激烈的论战，他们声称这种观点大错特错，纯属异想天开。但这些批评之声丝毫没有减损这部作品的声誉。相反，韦伯发人深省的思想观点和原创性的研究方法，使这部著作成为不朽的经典。

《新教伦理与资本主义精神》的学术价值

《新教伦理与资本主义精神》最重要的价值在于其观点和方法的原创性。它已成为社会学最具影响力的奠基性作品之一，甚至有人认为它就是最重要的巨著。学者们普遍认为，它是创造性地运用经验＊研究的一个范例，即通过观察或实验来证实或证伪的研究方法。韦伯著作的重要性无论怎样强调都不为过。

然而，这部作品的命运并不因其历史意义而一帆风顺；事实上，反对意见从未停歇。现代资本主义的发展已成为社会学的核心问题，因此它仍然具有现实意义。社会学的其他创始人，如 19 世纪的德国政治思想家卡尔·马克思 * 和法国社会学先驱埃米尔·迪尔克姆 * 也都研究过这个问题。有人认为，韦伯的观点是对马克思有关工业资本主义的"历史唯物主义" * 理论的批判。马克思强调社会的经济和阶级结构取决于物质生活条件，而韦伯与之相反，认为社会思想也非常重要。

除了社会学，《新教伦理与资本主义精神》也在各研究和分支领域引起了激烈的反响。例如，组织社会学 * 以正式和非正式组织为研究对象，深受韦伯对科层制 * 分析的影响，研究者以此来分析制度结构，以及制度如何决定个人行为。

虽然有些学者仍在质疑《新教伦理与资本主义精神》提出的观点，今天的社会学家还是更多地将其运用到新的研究中去。这部著作无疑被引用得最多，用来说明宗教信仰对工作态度的重要作用——这显然源自韦伯的主要观点，即某些新教教派的宗教信仰可以解释现代资本主义的产生。《新教伦理与资本主义精神》对社会的现代化和合理化 *（即社会生活逐渐受理性决策和假设支配的过程）问题的研究也具有重要影响。韦伯认为，合理化的过程——特别是工作的合理化——构成了导致现代资本主义的运动的重要特征。

---

1 玛丽安娜·韦伯：《马克斯·韦伯传》，哈里·左恩译，新泽西州新不伦瑞克：交易出版社，1988 年，第 335 页。

第一部分：学术渊源

1 作者生平与历史背景

要点 🔑

- 《新教伦理与资本主义精神》是一部革命性的著作，它旨在阐释现代资本主义*的发展。

- 韦伯与清教徒*的禁欲主义*——忘我——之间有着极大的亲和力。

- 韦伯力图阐释现代资本主义在 20 世纪初的发展。

为什么要读这部著作？

马克斯·韦伯的《新教伦理与资本主义精神》是 20 世纪最重要的社会学*著作之一。韦伯使用了经验*数据来进行论证（即数据可以通过观察来验证），许多人认为这对社会学学科的建立起到了巨大的作用。无论是因为它的方法还是韦伯的观点，《新教伦理与资本主义精神》都具有十分重要的意义。

韦伯提出，为什么不同的群体会采取不同的经济行为。另外两位社会学创始人，德国政治思想家卡尔·马克思*和法国思想家埃米尔·迪尔克姆*也提出过这个问题。韦伯认为，是特定的宗教观念决定了人们的经济行为和社会经济结构。这是对马克思"历史唯物主义"*理论的直接批判。历史唯物主义认为是物质条件决定了社会的经济体制，而韦伯坚持认为思想观念的作用不容忽视。

韦伯认为，某些新教团体的观念可以帮助解释现代资本主义*经济和社会制度产生与发展的原因，这对学术发展意义重大，影响深远。尽管批评者指出《新教伦理与资本主义精神》中有许多是经验之谈（指它的科学发现），但在讨论思想观念对现代资本主义发展的作用时，它仍然是被引用最多的作品之一。正如英国社会学家安东尼·吉登斯*所说："《新教伦理与资本主义精神》无疑是现代社会科学中最著名、也最有争议的作品之一。"[1]

> 韦伯终其一生都将自己视为负有使命的"资产阶级学者"。
>
> 凯兰·阿兰：《马克斯·韦伯批判性导读》

作者生平

马克斯·韦伯 1864 年出生于普鲁士*（位于今天的德国和波兰部分地区）爱尔福特，1920 年在德国慕尼黑去世。韦伯的父亲是德国政界的一位重要人物，他与父亲的关系比较紧张。他的母亲深受美国一神论*和英国基督教改革宗*的影响（两者都是新教神学思想*），对韦伯形成关于新教伦理的看法起了重要作用。她自由、积极的宗教思想启发了韦伯去探寻道德力量，使他意识到道德标准对人们行为方式的指导作用。

韦伯的学术背景主要集中在法学上，但他的博士论文研究的是经济和法律史。1894 年，他成为弗赖堡大学*的经济学教授，两年后在海德堡大学*担任经济学教授。1897 年韦伯的父亲去世，随后他因神经衰弱被迫中止了大部分教学工作。1903 年至 1905 年，他开始撰写《新教伦理与资本主义精神》，1904 年和 1905 年分两次发表于当时极具影响力的期刊《社会科学与社会政治学文献》*。[2] 1920 年，《新教伦理与资本主义精神》成书出版，并附有大量补充的注释，作为对批评者的回应。

这本书对韦伯来说也具有特别的意义，他本人非常认同他自己所描述的新教徒的道德观。虽然其他学者可能也持相同的观点，但韦伯本人与《新教伦理与资本主义精神》中的概念密切相关，这使他获得了其他人可能错过的重要思想。

创作背景

20世纪之交，德国（以及欧洲各地）正处于前现代向现代过渡的十字路口。工业化还未到达乡村，因此某些方面还停留在旧时代。另一方面，城市正在迅速工业化，代表着现代性和未来。这种差异激发了许多关于这一时期的研究。学者们质疑资本主义会把我们的生活引向何方，他们看得出这是一个市场高于传统观念、道德价值和人际关系的体系。在《新教伦理与资本主义精神》中，韦伯部分解释了现代资本主义社会是如何从传统的经济组织中发展出来的。

韦伯论文关心的另一个社会问题是歧视（或者说歧视知觉）。当时德国天主教徒认为他们在公务员职位中的人数不足，为了争取更大的比例而四处游说。韦伯认为，天主教徒较少从事商业和专业工作的原因不是出于歧视，而是他们以宗教为基础的文化观念。他认为罗马天主教文化不像新教那样适合从事商业。19世纪的法国历史学家亚历克西斯·德·托克维尔*曾在他的著作《美国的民主》中，提出过宗教对经济行为的影响。[3]但社会科学家还没有系统地研究过这个问题。这个实际问题促使韦伯写了一篇文章，这不仅有助于理解经济生活的社会基础，正如我们理解的那样，也是为了给当时的政策辩论出力。

1　马克斯·韦伯：《新教伦理与资本主义精神》，塔尔科特·帕森斯译，伦敦：劳德里奇出版社，2005 年，第 VII 页。

2　《社会科学与社会政治学文献》，由韦伯、维尔纳·桑巴特和埃德加·雅费创编，是当时德国的前沿学术期刊。

3　维克多·倪（倪志伟）、理查德·斯威德伯格：《资本主义论》，加州斯坦福：斯坦福大学出版社，2007 年，第 54 页。

2 学术背景

要点 🗝

- 韦伯写作《新教伦理与资本主义精神》之际,探讨现代资本主义*的发展是最重要的学术问题之一。

- 当时,深受马克思主义学说影响的观点占据主导地位,强调物质利益——阶级和经济——在社会结构中的作用。

- 韦伯向这种主流观点发起了挑战,他强调思想观念而非物质利益的作用。

著作语境

这一时期的德国社会科学家和历史学家对资本主义的起源和工业化进程非常感兴趣,而马克斯·韦伯的《新教伦理与资本主义精神》是这一研究领域最具意义的著作之一。

在政治思想和经济学方面,德国的学术环境与同时期的英国大不相同。功利主义*哲学根据其效果来判断一个行为是否"善",而理想主义*哲学则根据是否可感知和思考来判断"真"。英国社会学家*安东尼·吉登斯*说:"功利主义哲学和古典政治经济学在英国占主导的情况并没有出现在德国,德国深受理想主义哲学的影响,19世纪末又日益受到马克思主义的影响,所以一直与英国流行的两种思潮保持着距离。"[1]

卡尔·马克思*的分析方法,强调是物质利益而非思想观念——比如宗教和文化——决定了资本主义的发展,这种方法的影响力日益增长。但理想主义在当时的德国仍占主导地位,根据

其唯心主义原则，人类行为不能简单地用因果关系来解释，而是
"必须以一种自然界其他物种身上不存在的方式去'解释'或'理
解'。"[2] 这种方法强调在历史中理解人类的行为，因为"赋予人类
生命意义的文化价值观……是由社会发展的特定过程创造的。"[3]

> （韦伯）是社会政治联盟*的"新生代"成员之一，
> 他们最早接触马克思主义理论的复杂图景，试图创造性地
> 运用马克思主义的某些思想，但并不全盘接受其理论体系，
> 也不赞同革命政治。
>
> 安东尼·吉登斯:《〈新教伦理与资本主义精神〉导读》

学科概览

在韦伯同时代人看来，马克思主义经济学家和社会学家维尔
纳·桑巴特*是研究现代资本主义发展的最重要学者之一。发表韦
伯论文《新教伦理与资本主义精神》的期刊，就是由桑巴特与他人
共同主编的。1902 年他出版了自己的代表作《现代资本主义》。在
《新教伦理与资本主义精神》中，韦伯与桑巴特《现代资本主义》
中的观点进行了正面交锋。

桑巴特运用马克思的历史唯物主义*来描述资本主义如何从封
建主义*演变而来（封建主义是中世纪的社会制度，其主要特征是
由土地所有权决定地位和财富）。他将资本主义划分为三个时期：早
期资本主义在 18 世纪中叶工业革命*开始之前就已结束，中期资本
主义始于 18 世纪中叶，晚期资本主义则始于第一次世界大战*之前。
1911 年桑巴特继续研究并写出了《犹太人与现代资本主义》（1913）。

与同时代的许多思想家一样，桑巴特认为，德国和欧洲其他地

区现代资本主义产生的主要原因是物质利益，而不是思想观念。尽管学术思想相左，他也有一些与韦伯的新教伦理假设相同的基本观点——尤其是宗教信仰可以影响工作习惯。此外，学界和受过教育的公众也认同宗教和职业地位之间存在着一定的关系。1902年，当讨论到新教加尔文主义*教派*与资本主义发展之间的关系时，桑巴特说这是"一个众所周知、毋庸置疑的事实"。[4]但是，社会科学家并没有认真研究这种关系，直到韦伯发起了挑战。在1920年出版的《新教伦理与资本主义精神》附加注释以及其他著述中，韦伯对桑巴特和其他评论家进行了回应。

学术渊源

1896年来到海德堡*之后，韦伯遇到了许多重要的哲学家和社会科学家。他们成为韦伯学术圈的一部分，其中包括格奥尔格·耶利内克*、恩斯特·特勒尔奇*（他们都对《新教伦理与资本主义精神》产生过影响）、维尔纳·桑巴特以及后来成为韦伯妻子的社会学家、女权活动家玛丽安娜·韦伯*等学者。在马克斯·韦伯的影响下，还有许多学者也慕名来到海德堡。其中最重要的一位，是现在几乎被遗忘的德国经济学家和历史学家埃伯哈德·哥赛因*。虽然韦伯的学术圈并没有形成统一的思想流派，但其中一些成员对《新教伦理与资本主义精神》产生过重大影响。除了桑巴特，韦伯还与另一位共同创办了《社会科学与社会政治学文献》期刊的埃德加·雅费进行论战。恩斯特·特勒尔奇将有关加尔文主义的社会学读物引介给韦伯。最重要的可能是埃伯哈德·哥赛因，正是他的《黑森林经济史》（1892），使韦伯注意到加尔文主义在资本主义传播中的作用。不过韦伯曾回忆说，他是受到耶利内克《人权和公

14

民权宣言》的启发才重新"开始研究清教徒"的。[5] 耶利内克激发韦伯去注意宗教的影响——而这并不是资本主义研究学者的常规思路。

对韦伯产生重要影响的学者还有新康德主义者 *——18 世纪德国哲学家伊曼纽尔·康德哲学的追随者,特别是 1903 年他开始研究社会学的认识论基础(即思想观念对社会形成的作用)的时期。其中最著名的是海因里希·里克特 *、威廉·温德尔班德 *、威廉·狄尔泰 * 和格奥尔格·西梅尔 *。这些哲学家区分了人文科学和实证主义 * 的自然科学;对于实证主义者来说,只有能被经验证实的知识才有效。韦伯和西梅尔创立了诠释社会学 *,或称理解社会学,与法国实证主义社会学形成鲜明对比。它试图通过理解行为的主观意义——例如新教徒工作的意义——来解释行动的原因和结果,而不仅仅是描述事实。

1　马克斯·韦伯:《新教伦理与资本主义精神》,塔尔科特·帕森斯译,伦敦:劳德里奇出版社,2005 年,第 VIII 页。

2　马克斯·韦伯:《新教伦理与资本主义精神》,第 IX 页。

3　马克斯·韦伯:《新教伦理与资本主义精神》,第 IX 页。

4　马克斯·韦伯:《经济与社会》,冈瑟·罗斯、克劳斯·威特奇主编,加州伯克利:加利福尼亚大学出版社,1978 年,第 LXXVI 页。

5　马克斯·韦伯:《新教伦理与资本主义"精神"》,彼得·贝尔、戈登·威尔斯译,纽约:企鹅出版社,2002 年,第 155 页。

3 主导命题

要点 ☐━

- 韦伯时代的研究集中在影响现代资本主义 * 发展的各种因素。
- 主要观点集中在物质或理性 * 因素，也包括某些文化群体的作用。
- 在《新教伦理与资本主义精神》中，韦伯提出了一个观点，即某些新教 * 教派 * 的信仰观念对现代资本主义的发展有重大影响。

核心问题

在《新教伦理与资本主义精神》中，马克斯·韦伯试图回答两个核心问题。第一个问题是，在某些新教信仰和"职业伦理"（亦即"工作伦理"）之间是否存在明确的"选择性亲和力" *（一种天然联系或因果关系）。韦伯主要是指新教伦理与"资本主义精神"之间是否存在亲和力。他所指的"资本主义精神"是一种追逐财富、利润和物质成功的生活方式。这种对工作和经济收益永无止境的追求，没有发生在前现代的"传统"社会经济中。对前现代文化而言，工作是不得已的事，闲暇更有意义，因此人们只是为了满足传统需求而被迫工作。

这个核心思想直接回答了现代资本主义如何产生的问题。韦伯的论述反驳了受马克思主义的唯物史观 * 影响——强调经济利益的重要作用。他研究如何用特定群体的特定观念来解释现代资本主义的发展。

韦伯的第二个问题也与现代资本主义的发展有关。他想探讨"我们现代生活的核心特征有多少源自宗教改革 *（16 世纪基督新

16

教兴起的运动）带来的宗教力量，又有多少源自其他。"[1] 这个问题可以用来解释资本主义兴起所带来的巨大文化变革，尤其是人们在现代社会中的经济行为变化。

> 俗谚谑称："要么吃得香，要么睡得稳"。现在，新教徒想要吃得香，而天主教徒只想睡得稳。
>
> 马克斯·韦伯:《新教伦理与资本主义精神》

参与者

马克斯·韦伯写作《新教伦理与资本主义精神》时，主流的经济史学术研究都不承认宗教会影响经济伦理。传统研究认为，现代资本主义源于物质利益和权力、历史演变和进步、犹太人的商业交易，以及抽象的理性主义（产生了现代社会的理性思维和理性行为）等等。例如，维尔纳·桑巴特*强调犹太人在资本主义兴起中所起的作用。他还认为，资本主义是社会理性发展的一个特殊阶段。其他采用马克思主义视角的研究，则从阶级利益的角度看待资本主义的产生。

经济史学家不会去系统解释经济行为的主观"意义"，韦伯在他早期的作品中也没有这样做过。事实上，专业的历史学家很少去研究文化史。历史学家埃伯哈德·哥赛因*——1904 年韦伯请他到海德堡*大学接替自己的经济史教授职务——是极少数例外中的一员。哥赛因指出，新教加尔文主义*对资本主义的传播有一定帮助。宗教改革使中世纪罗马天主教分裂，基督新教兴起并产生了加尔文主义和其他新教教派，韦伯详细分析了各阶段宗教信仰与资本主义之间的特定关系，进一步发展了哥赛因的观点。

于是，《新教伦理与资本主义精神》突破了主流经济史研究的窠臼，融入了德国的新兴学科——社会学 *。这部著作专注于对意义的解释，成为德国"诠释社会学"*的基础之一。这是由韦伯和社会学先驱、哲学家格奥尔格·西梅尔共同创立的社会学理论。

当代论战

在《新教伦理与资本主义精神》中，韦伯对有关现代资本主义兴起的各种理论予以关注。他反对桑巴特的进化论，事实上这也是韦伯撰写这篇论文的主要动机之一。与桑巴特的观点不同，韦伯认为事物的变化并不是在所有领域并行发展的。基于古罗马正义原则的法律出现在中世纪 *，但在英国发展起来的现代资本主义却伴随着一种形式上不那么理性的法律——普通法 *。这就打破了桑巴特的观点。[2] 与马克思主义的观点相反，韦伯认为"资本主义精神"先于美国资产阶级（企业主构成的中产阶级）存在。在他看来，资本主义并不是由商业精英，而是由中产阶级新兴企业家滋生出来的。因此，资本主义的产生就不可能用单一的阶级理论来解释。[3]

《新教伦理与资本主义精神》也受到各学科研究者的极大关注，最重要的批评来自历史学家费利克斯·拉赫福尔 *和卡尔·菲舍尔 *。他们于 1907 年和 1909 年分别在两种期刊上发表了评论文章。韦伯对这两篇文章和其他一些批评进行了激烈的反驳。他认为，他们缺乏对这个主题的了解，无法完全理解他的作品。1911年至 1916 年间，经济学家维尔纳·桑巴特——他也是一位社会学家，和路约·布伦塔诺 *也在其论著中批评了《新教伦理与资本主义精神》。韦伯在 1920 年出版的《新教伦理与资本主义精神》一书中补充了新的注释给予回击。他为自己做了一些澄清，但从未改变过其最初的观点。

　　社会学家对《新教伦理与资本主义精神》毁誉参半，其他学科的研究者则是更多地给予批评，包括历史学、经济学、心理学，甚至文学评论界。许多评论家批评韦伯的观点缺乏准确的经验*，比如他引用美国革命家本杰明·富兰克林*的著作作为论据。⁴尽管如此，每一个研究现代资本主义起源的学者，如果希望自己的观点能进入学术论战的中心，都无法绕过"韦伯命题"。

1　马克斯·韦伯：《新教伦理与资本主义精神》，斯蒂芬·卡尔伯格译，纽约：牛津大学出版社，2009 年第 4 版，第 XXVIII 页。

2　弗里茨·林格：《韦伯学术思想评传》，芝加哥：芝加哥大学出版社，2010 年，第 117 页。

3　林格：《韦伯学术思想评传》，第 115 页。

4　林格：《韦伯学术思想评传》，第 125 页。

4 作者贡献

要点 ⚷——

- 韦伯认为，宗教观念对经济行为产生影响，可以用来解释现代资本主义经济和社会制度的形成。

- 韦伯之前也有人涉及这个主题，但他是第一个用宗教观念来解释现代资本主义的思想家。

- 韦伯的写作回应了马克思主义经济学家和社会学家维尔纳·桑巴特*的研究观点，他分别受到了法律哲学家格奥尔格·耶利内克*和文化历史学家埃伯哈德·哥赛因论著的影响。

作者目标

在写作《新教伦理与资本主义精神》时，马克斯·韦伯对一些既有的解释现代资本主义产生的理论持怀疑态度。这些理论大多认为，文化价值观"通常是从属于社会结构、权力、阶级、社会变革以及经济和政治利益的被动力量"。维尔纳·桑巴特在《现代资本主义》（1902）中就明确提出过这种观点。韦伯对部分伟大人物推动历史发展这一叙述也持保留意见。[1]

韦伯使用"资本主义精神"*这一术语来说明西方资本主义的具体形式。正如他所看到的，为了更好地追求利润，西方资本主义以理性和精打细算的方式组织劳动。他认为，"资本主义精神"作为一种世俗*的"伦理导向"，指向一种系统性的"生活方式"，以财富、利润、工作、竞争和物质成功为其终极目标。[2] 为了理解资本主义的起源，韦伯认为我们应该研究其精神的起源。这种精神在新教徒*中似乎十分普遍。因此，韦伯希望进一步研究宗教信仰是否以及如何产生了这种精神。

> 理性化和智识化是我们时代的宿命，一切都是为了世界的祛魅。
>
> 马克斯·韦伯：《科学作为天职》

研究方法

为了研究现代资本主义是如何产生的，韦伯考察文化价值如何决定社会的经济结构——过去这是一种边缘化的研究方法。韦伯大规模地调查特定的行为动机，希望揭示"社会行为的主观意义"。这也成为他整个历史解释研究中的核心方法。韦伯创立了诠释社会学*，或称理解社会学，而不使用实证主义*和经济决定论*的方法来理解社会现象。对实证主义者来说，只有可以通过经验验证的知识才有效；经济决定论认为，经济关系是解释社会现象的基础（这是与经典马克思主义相关的观点）。

通过研究新教徒和罗马天主教徒行为背后的意义及宗教原因，韦伯成为最先解释新教徒与罗马天主教徒之间经济行为差异的思想家之一。他认为，用既存的物质条件无法解释德国某些地区普遍存在的经济行为选择。比如，新教徒为什么普遍比罗马天主教徒更富有；[3] 又比如，为什么罗马天主教徒倾向于选择人文科目，而新教徒更青睐商业课程。韦伯认为，显然是宗教信仰在决定人们的经济行为方面发挥了重要作用，他认为这是很值得认真研究的。他的研究方法对当时流行的受马克思主义影响的理论学说发起了挑战，传统理论认为物质（主要指经济）决定了社会形态。

时代贡献

　　新教教义与资本主义存在因果关系的观点与当时的主流学术观点不同，但这并不是韦伯第一个发现的。他指出，西班牙人早就发现了荷兰加尔文宗 * 与其贸易发展之间的联系，英国经济学家威廉·佩蒂爵士 * 也提出过类似的主张。[4]经济史学家埃伯哈德·哥赛因 * 把加尔文主义侨民 *——加尔文主义者向各国扩散——描写为"资本主义经济的苗床"，[5]这对韦伯研究产生了重要的影响。

　　韦伯还对维尔纳·桑巴特的研究作出过回应。在《现代资本主义》（1902）中，桑巴特提出是资本主义的物质条件创造了新教教派 * 的观点，[6]韦伯则认为桑巴特颠倒了因果。在韦伯看来，现代资本主义起源于新教教义中的"资本主义精神"。另一位较早关注宗教对资本主义影响的学者是法律哲学家格奥尔格·耶利内克 *。韦伯对清教徒 * 的研究直接受到了耶利内克在《人权和公民权宣言》（1895）中观点的影响。耶利内克、桑巴特、哥赛因以及其他一些学者，都是后来被称为"韦伯学术圈"的成员。尽管没有形成一个思想流派，但许多成员都对韦伯关于现代资本主义发展的思考产生了影响。

1　马克斯·韦伯：《新教伦理与资本主义精神》，斯蒂芬·卡尔伯格译，纽约：牛津大学出版社，2009 年第 4 版，第 XXV—VI 页。

2 马克斯·韦伯:《新教伦理与资本主义精神》,斯蒂芬·卡尔伯格译,第 17 页。

3 马克斯·韦伯:《新教伦理与资本主义精神》,塔尔科特·帕森斯译,伦敦:劳德里奇出版社,2005 年,第 4 页。

4 马克斯·韦伯:《新教伦理与资本主义精神》,第 10 页。

5 马克斯·韦伯:《新教伦理与资本主义精神》,第 10 页。

6 维尔纳·桑巴特:《现代资本主义》,无英译版。

第二部分：学术思想

5 思想主脉

要点 ⚸

- 韦伯研究的核心主题是"资本主义精神"*，起源于某些新教*教派*，以及如何用宗教观念来解释现代资本主义*的产生。

- 韦伯认为，通过研究路德宗*和加尔文主义*教派如何影响人的行为，我们可以解释理性化*、世俗*和"现代"的资本主义。

- 《新教伦理与资本主义精神》第一部分提出问题，第二部分分析问题。

核心主题

韦伯发现新教徒比罗马天主教徒*更富有，更多地参与商业活动，并开始在《新教伦理和资本主义精神》中展开论证。他指出："商业领袖和资本所有者、高级熟练工以及现代企业的技术和商业员工，几乎都是新教徒。"[1]韦伯由此产生一个重要假设：新教徒，特别是加尔文主义者和马丁·路德*——宗教改革中创立基督新教的关键人物——的信徒，他们的宗教经济伦理与资本主义高度吻合。

并不是任何时代都有对经济伦理的系统研究和对利润的理性追求，但它早在现代资本主义产生之前就在西方出现了。对韦伯来说，这表明很有可能是"资本主义精神"激发了现代资本主义的发展。

韦伯描述了加尔文宗和其他新教教派中体现"资本主义精神"的基本思想，比如约翰·加尔文*的预定论*。加尔文——16世纪的法国神学家*——指出，哪些人能上天堂是上帝预定的，与人们的现世作为无关。韦伯认为这种观点让虔诚的信徒陷入绝望："一个人的内心感受到前所未有的孤独。"[2] 后来，加尔文主义神学家（研究宗教思想和经文的学者）修改了这条教义：那些兢兢业业将禁欲*工作（杜绝物质享受的忘我工作）视为天职*、合理追求利润的人最终能得救赎。这给信徒带来了巨大的心理安慰。

16 世纪的德国神父马丁·路德提出了"天职"的概念，声称"每个人都有上帝赋予他或她的'召唤'或'职业'"。[3] 韦伯认为这解释了为什么新教徒更有可能变得富裕，更愿意从事商业。

通过总体分析新教伦理与资本主义的历史联系，韦伯得出了结论。他认为禁欲工作的风气在后来成为美国的 18 世纪新大陆生根发芽，但在这个新的国家，禁欲精神被世俗化了。资本主义脱离了它的宗教精神基础，社会走向理性，人们别无选择，只能接受资本主义："现在，追求利润已经不是为了恩慈，而是因为它符合自身利益。"[4]

> 一般而言，即使有良好的意愿，现代人也无法对塑造其文化和民族性格的宗教给予足够的重视。但至少不能用单一的唯物主义来取代同样单一的文化历史决定论。
>
> 马克斯·韦伯：《新教伦理与资本主义精神》

思想探究

《新教伦理与资本主义精神》提出了三个原创且相互关联的观点。第一，源于新教伦理的资本主义"精神"作用巨大；第二，路德的天职观、加尔文的预定论激发人们从事禁欲工作、追求利润；第三，18 世纪以来，新教伦理出现了世俗化，尤其是在美国。以上观点形成了"韦伯命题"的核心：新教伦理是现代资本主义产生的驱动力，但这种显著的联系今天已消失殆尽。

韦伯认为，如果没有"资本主义精神"中所包含的这种职业伦理，人们只是为了生存而工作。[5] 路德天职观中的新教伦理是把"日常生活中的劳动视为上帝赋予的任务"。[6] 路德的"尘世工作"与罗马天主教僧侣的逃避禁欲形成了鲜明对比。

那些接受加尔文主义和其他新教教派禁欲伦理的人，与资本主义之间建立了一种更为紧密的"内在亲和力"。他们在天职中勤奋工作，获得成功。加尔文教义中最初的预定论让信徒感到无比痛苦，但那些深信自己被拣选的人，通过投身于天职，在禁欲工作中获得了巨大的心理满足。韦伯之前，其他学者也曾注意到加尔文主义与资本主义之间的关系，但他们没有进一步具体分析。

18世纪，禁欲工作的风气在美国以一种世俗化的方式出现。美国革命政治家本杰明·富兰克林*的刻苦工作、商业活动和道德品行，就是一个典型的例子。比如，富兰克林提出"时间就是金钱"，[7] 强调金融活动中的行为应该正当："记住，善付款者是他人钱袋的主人。"[8] 禁欲工作和财富不再为个人换来救赎，而是社区公民应当具备的高尚品德。韦伯由此得出结论，在革命时代的美国，"获得胜利的资本主义"已不再需要那种将工作视为天职的观念。一旦大批企业家以现代资本主义的方式组织生产，将迫使每个人要么加入竞争，要么自取灭亡。

学者们运用韦伯的观点来强调文化——特别是宗教——在工作取向和动机中的重要作用。他的思想也说明了新教与资本主义和更广泛的理性主义*之间的关系。理性化*（越来越多地采用计算行为达到特定目标的过程）的概念，解释了为什么最初受宗教教义影响的社会行为在世俗社会中也能继续存在。

语言表述

韦伯写作《新教伦理与资本主义精神》，将目标对准了德国的社会科学家和历史学家，他们引发了关于资本主义和工业主义起源的学术论战。韦伯以学术风格写作，大量使用专业术语，因为他不需要吸引外行。例如，韦伯不使用"自由意志"一词，而是使用拉丁语的 liberum arbitrium。但是这本书也并不晦涩。他使用什么样的语言可能只是与他的创作时代有关，与他的读者没太大关系。

韦伯的《新教伦理与资本主义精神》分为两个部分，第一部分简要介绍了研究的问题及其相关性，第二部分是分析和结论。

韦伯著名的"铁笼" * 一词，最早出现在 1930 年社会学家 * 塔尔科特·帕森斯 * 翻译的《新教伦理与资本主义精神》英文版中。韦伯使用德语 "stahlhartes Gehiiuse"，即"铁笼"，来描述西方日益理性化的社会和经济生活。也有一些批评者认为，比"铁笼"更准确的翻译可能是"钢铁般的外壳"。[9]

---

1 马克斯·韦伯：《新教伦理与资本主义精神》，塔尔科特·帕森斯译，伦敦：劳德里奇出版社，2005 年，第 3 页。

2 马克斯·韦伯：《新教伦理与资本主义精神》，第 60 页。

3 凯兰·阿兰：《马克斯·韦伯评述》，普卢托出版社，2004 年，第 36 页。

4 劳拉·德斯弗·伊德勒斯：《古典时代的社会学理论：文本与阅读》，第 3 版，千橡市，加州：世哲出版社，2014 年，第 166 页。

5 马克斯·韦伯：《新教伦理与资本主义精神》，第 24 页。

6　凯兰·阿兰:《马克斯·韦伯评述》,第36页。

7　马克斯·韦伯:《新教伦理与资本主义精神》,第14页。

8　马克斯·韦伯:《新教伦理与资本主义精神》,第15页。

9　彼得·贝尔:《"铁笼"和"钢铁般的外壳":帕森斯与韦伯的隐喻》,载《历史与理论》,总40期,2001年第2期,第153—169页。

6 思想支脉

要点 ⚷—

- 韦伯的观点引发学者们对卡尔·马克思*等强调物质作用的历史理论开展批评，他们研究文化对经济发展的贡献，阐明了预定论*在资本主义*产生过程中发挥的作用。
- 韦伯的研究打破了马克思主义理论在当时的主导地位。
- 韦伯关于预定论与现代资本主义产生有密切关联的观点影响巨大，它为"韦伯命题"奠定了基础。

其他思想

马克斯·韦伯在《新教伦理与资本主义精神》中还提出了一系列次要观点来支持他的主要思想，其中有许多对社会学*理论产生了显著影响。韦伯认为，资本主义本身并不能创造出"资本主义精神"。*学者们运用这一定义来批评历史唯物主义*强调经济而忽视观念，比如卡尔·马克思。韦伯还说，即使资本主义能传播其"精神"，也一定有某种力量在推动人们有系统地追求利润。这种观念必须有一个群体、一个组织或者一个阶级，来成为它的"社会载体"。[1]这是韦伯提出的另一个具有影响力的观点。

韦伯认为，新教徒*与罗马天主教徒*既存的物质财富差异，并不能完全解释他们之间经济成就的差异。这种观点影响了文化主义者对不平等和贫困的解释——他们考察文化因素对物质环境的影响。例如，有人指出，对经济行为的文化态度不同，世界各地的发展水平也不同。[2]德国经济学家萨沙·贝克尔*认为，韦伯对新教和罗马天主教态度的分析，甚至可以帮助理解欧元区＊（以欧元为货币的欧洲部分地区）的当代经济问题。³ 信奉新教的北欧国家普遍比信奉罗马天主教的地中海国家财政更加稳健。根据这种观点，文化态度造成这些国家经济状况也不尽相同。文化态度发生冲突，政治危机也随之而来。

> 我们可以清楚地看到预定论对这一时代人们的行为方式和生活态度造成的影响，尽管它作为教条的权威正在衰落。
>
> 马克斯·韦伯:《新教伦理与资本主义精神》

思想探究

韦伯提出的最重要的次要思想是救赎观念（基督教教义，指上帝从永恒的诅咒中拯救有价值的东西）的社会影响，特别是其带来的经济结果。这也成为韦伯后来的宗教社会学著作中的一个核心要素，具有深远的影响。他梳理了罗马天主教、路德宗＊、加尔文宗＊和基督新教各宗派的救赎问题。天主教徒认为忏悔可以使罪孽得到宽恕，甚至罪人也可以获得救赎。但新教各派对罪孽的态度十分强硬——尤其是加尔文宗，强调预定论（个人灵魂的命运完全由上帝预先决定）。那么他们如何缓解那些担心救恩的信徒的焦虑呢？他们把理性工作的概念转换为天职＊——上帝赋予的使命，这就给以前看来平淡无奇的工作带来了宗教意义。

加尔文的"预定论"让信徒陷入绝望，因为他们无法知道和控制自己灵魂的最终命运。所以后来的神学家＊和基督教牧师，其中包括虔敬派＊、循道宗＊、贵格会＊和浸礼会＊，重新解释了这条教义。他们指出，获得拯救的人主要有四种品质：第一，有条不紊的工作能力；第二，创造财富和利润的能力；第三，保持纯洁（遵循美德）；第四，感受到与上帝同在。[4] 这些特征给那些恪守禁欲工作生活方式的人们带来了极大的安慰。

英国社会学家肯·莫里森解释了这种观点如何使得"新教徒倾向于与世界保持距离"。[5] 新教徒走上了一条上帝赐予的孤独的救赎之路，丝毫不受外界的影响。[6] 另外，苦行僧般的工作也让他对自己的生活方式感到"格外满足"，由此而形成的经济行为影响了资本主义的产生。[7] 因此，加尔文的教义不仅影响了信徒们的行为，也为现代资本主义的产生奠定了基础。

忽视之处

马克斯·韦伯的《新教伦理与资本主义精神》是社会科学中争议最多的作品之一，从中很难找到还没有引起注意的观点。学者们已经反复研究了其主要和次要的思想，它的许多观点还启发了完全不同的学科领域的研究，学者们似乎已经穷尽了一切可能的研究应用。

然而，有些观点引起的关注甚至超出了韦伯的预期，而且被赋予了新的意义。其中最典型的例子是关于"铁笼"的比喻，即西方资本主义的合理化给个人生活套上了一个"铁笼"。著名社会学家塔尔科特·帕森斯*1930 年翻译此书时创造了这个词，这是第一个英译版，后来也成为了经典。但是最近的翻译家批评了他的用词，他们认为，韦伯的"stahlhartes Gehiiuse"应该翻译为"钢铁般的外壳"[8]，或者"钢铁般坚硬的外壳"[9] 才更为精确。尽管如此，帕森斯的概念已经取得了自己的特殊意义和共鸣，在很大程度上独立于韦伯使用这一隐喻的背景。它出现在数百种社会学著述中，学者们还经常将其应用于其他主题，比如组织分析。[10]

1　马克斯·韦伯：《新教伦理与资本主义精神》，斯蒂芬·卡尔伯格译，第4版，纽约：牛津大学出版社，2009年，第XXV—VI页。

2　劳伦斯·哈里森、萨缪尔·亨廷顿：《文化的重要作用：价值观如何影响人类进步》，纽约：基本图书出版社，2000年。

3　克里斯·阿诺特：《新教与基督教：哪种国家更成功？》，载2011年10月31日《卫报》，登录日期2015年9月5日。

4　马克斯·韦伯：《新教伦理与资本主义精神》，第XXXV页。

5　肯·莫里森：《马克思、迪尔克姆、韦伯：现代社会思想的奠基人》，伦敦：世哲出版社，2006年，第322页

6　肯·莫里森：《马克思、迪尔克姆、韦伯：现代社会思想的奠基人》，第322页

7　肯·莫里森：《马克思、迪尔克姆、韦伯：现代社会思想的奠基人》，第324页

8　马克斯·韦伯：《新教伦理与资本主义精神》，第158页。

9　马克斯·韦伯：《新教伦理与资本主义"精神"》，彼得·贝尔、戈登·威尔斯译，纽约：企鹅出版社，2002年，第121页。

10　詹姆斯·巴克：《收紧铁笼：自我管理型团队的协调控制》，载《管理科学季刊》总38期，1993年第3期，第408—437页。

7 历史成就

要点 🔑━

- 《新教伦理与资本主义精神》深刻影响了社会学 * 的创立。
- 韦伯运用经验 * 方法有力证明了宗教信仰对经济行为的影响。
- 韦伯的观点今天看来可能并不可靠，因为 20 世纪之交的韦伯不可能像今天的研究者那样获得更多和更广泛的经验材料。

观点评价

　　凭借其极具原创性的论点，马克斯·韦伯的《新教伦理与资本主义精神》一直是社会科学领域最受争议、最著名的作品之一。实际上，学者们公认其为社会学的奠基之作，也是经验主义社会学研究方法的典范。然而，有些学者认为韦伯并未全部完成自己的研究，也有学者批评"韦伯命题"的论据。例如，德国经济学家萨沙·贝克尔 * 和卢德格尔·沃斯曼因 * 认为，新教徒的经济成功并非源于新教的职业道德，也可能是因为新教徒的文化程度更高。[1]当然，也得为韦伯说句话，贝克尔和沃斯曼因这些现代学者今天能获得的数据远比他当时的多。

　　但是我们决不能说，《新教伦理与资本主义精神》的学术价值仅仅在于其缜密的经验主义研究，它为德国乃至西欧以及美国围绕现代资本主义的产生而引发的学术争议也作出了贡献。韦伯批评卡尔·马克思的著名论断，即物质（主要是经济）因素是历史进步的主要驱动力，他认为历史发展没有既定法则，这一点后来得到许多重要学者的赞同。

> 写于 1904 年至 1905 年的《新教伦理和资本主义精神》，
> 可能是 20 世纪最重要的社会学著述。
>
> 丹尼尔·贝尔:《新教伦理与资本主义精神述评》

当时的成就

1904 年和 1905 年，《新教伦理与资本主义精神》系列论文在很有影响力的《社会科学与社会政治学文献》*期刊上发表。韦伯和马克思主义经济学家、社会学家维尔纳·桑巴特一起担任期刊的主编。由于这是德国最知名、最有声望的学术期刊之一，韦伯的论文很快引起了关注。但是《新教伦理与资本主义精神》只有德语版，直到 1930 年塔尔科特·帕森斯*将它翻译成英语，这就意味着英语学界在 25 年之后才看到它，但这似乎丝毫没能影响它的学术地位。

任何经验主义的论证都会因为新证据的出现而引起争议。例如，意大利德裔经济学家达维德·坎托尼*指出，新教与经济增长没有任何关系:"使用 1300 年至 1900 年间 272 个城市的人口数据，我们发现新教对经济增长并没有影响。这一发现的数据精确，各种控制因素总体稳定，并不依赖于数据选择和小规模样本。"[2] 也有学者提出证据支持韦伯的观点。经济学家乌尔里希·布鲁姆*和莱昂纳德·达德利*指出，1500 年至 1750 年间罗马天主教*城市的工资水平下降，而新教城市的工资水平提升。[3] 然而，《新教伦理与资本主义精神》的学术价值并不仅仅取决于其经验论证的准确性。

局限性

韦伯写作《新教伦理与资本主义精神》的动机之一，是为了理

36

解和解释西方理性化 *（社会行为日益受到理性决策和理性行为支配的过程）的根源。韦伯认为"西方的合理化是通过他称之为计算的过程推进的"。[4] 这意味着当经济价值开始在日常生活中发挥更大的作用，用货币来衡量一切能使人更好地控制物质世界。[5] 韦伯用合理化过程，来说明在西欧和美国出现的资本主义具体形态。从这个意义上说，我们得承认《新教伦理与资本主义精神》只能帮助我们分析西欧和美国的经济状况。

虽然韦伯确信新教伦理是现代资本主义产生的催化剂，但他并不认为它是唯一的催化剂。因此，《新教伦理与资本主义精神》在欧洲和美国之外也具有适用性，因为它指出了宗教与经济行为之间的潜在关系。韦伯在他的"世界诸宗教的经济伦理"[6] 研究系列中讨论了这个问题——在《经济与社会》（1921）[7] 和《一般经济史》（1923）中作了进一步讨论。最值得注意的是，他分析了为什么现代资本主义没有出现在印度和中国，他考察了这两个国家的宗教和经济伦理的作用、物质条件、法律和司法系统等各种因素。

然而，有些学者，比如美国人类学 * 和地理学教授詹姆斯·布劳特 *，批评韦伯的观点是欧洲中心论 *（即，认为欧洲经验和视角优先）。在他看来，韦伯也持有欧洲例外的观点——认为欧洲在某种程度上是一个"特例"——而高估了西方理性主义 * 或"资本主义精神"的独特性。[8] 学者们还批评韦伯总是将经济落后归因于其他文化。很多时候他忽略或低估了那些非西方的文化元素，他也没有说明欧洲殖民主义压迫某些本土文化的事实。

1　萨沙·贝克尔、卢德格尔·沃斯曼:《韦伯错了吗？——新教经济史的人力资本理论》,哈佛大学教育政策与治理研究项目,2007年。

2　达维德·坎托尼:《新教改革对经济的影响》,载《欧洲经济学会期刊》总13期,2014年第4期,第561页。

3　乌尔里希·布卢姆、伦纳德·达德利:《宗教与经济增长》,载《进化经济学》总11期,2001年第2期,第207—230页。

4　肯·莫里森:《马克思、迪尔克姆、韦伯:现代社会思想的奠基人》,伦敦:世哲出版社,2006年,第284页。

5　莫里森:《马克思、迪尔克姆、韦伯》,第284—285页。

6　韦伯在1911—1914年间一直从事这方面研究,但未能全部完成。1920年德国出版的《宗教社会学论文集》收录了他的研究,其中包括《新教伦理与资本主义精神》、《中国的宗教》(1915)、《印度的宗教》(1916)、《古犹太教》(1917)和《世界诸宗教的经济伦理观》(1920)。

7　马克斯·韦伯:《经济与社会》,冈瑟·罗斯、克劳斯·威特奇主编,伯克利:加利福尼亚大学出版社,1978年。

8　J. M. 布劳特:《八种欧洲中心论历史学家》,纽约:吉尔福德出版社,2002年,第29页。

8 著作地位

要点 🔑

- 韦伯终生致力于研究西方资本主义*的发展。
- 《新教伦理与资本主义精神》是韦伯的首次尝试。
- 《新教伦理与资本主义精神》使韦伯成为 20 世纪最具影响力的思想家之一。

定位

《新教伦理与资本主义精神》是马克斯·韦伯研究成熟阶段的第一个代表作。这一时期他从神经衰弱中恢复过来，研究转向了诠释社会学*：这种方法并不强调描述客观事实，而是通过理解其主观意义来解释行动的原因和结果。1905 年《新教伦理与资本主义精神》发表后，韦伯在其论文《新教教派与资本主义精神》（1906）中继续研究宗教对经济行为和社会结构的影响。受到 1904 年美国之行的启发，他在文中分析了 20 世纪初美国新教与资本主义之间的关系。

韦伯指出，新教在美国促进了资本主义的发展。他把这归因于新教教派*的预定论*思想产生的心理诱因（他说，人们行动得好像自己是被拣选的，这样才更能忍受生活的艰辛），但这种诱因也同样存在于欧洲。韦伯认为，美国的新教教会还形成了一种特定的群体规范，强化了经济行为的道德性，有助于资本主义的发展。这些规范包括按时还款、定价公道。韦伯在美国看到的这种行为，为资本主义精神向世俗*的职业道德转变铺平了道路；这种职业道德最终成为整个社会的规范，而不仅限于某些新教教派。

发表了美国新教教派的论文之后，韦伯又开始进一步研究最初的命题。首先，他跳出基督教，扩大范围进行比较研究。1911年至1914年，他开始了"世界诸宗教的经济伦理"系列。通过考察印度教*、佛教*、儒教*、道教*和犹太教*（一种源自中东的宗教）等非西方宗教，韦伯研究了各种宗教如何塑造信徒的经济行为方式。他认为，这解释了为什么资本主义没有在西方之外产生，特别是没有在印度和中国。

> 《新教伦理与资本主义精神》是韦伯出版的第一部著作，也成为他研究的核心成果。
> 肯·莫里斯《马克思、迪尔克姆和韦伯：现代社会学三大奠基人》

整合

《新教伦理与资本主义精神》出版之后，韦伯开始关注可能导致资本主义产生和西方合理化进程的其他因素。*他并不认为宗教可以完全解释现代资本主义的产生。相反，他强调物质条件也起着重要的作用。韦伯在《经济与社会》（1921）和《一般经济史》（1923）中继续研究西方资本主义的兴起。

他认为，许多其他因素也在西方资本主义的产生中发挥了重要作用。比如理性计算*和定价策略，以及可量刑的法律体系。所有这些都是与西方资本主义几乎同时产生的。如果将西方与世界其他地区进行比较，那么这些非宗教因素的重要性就更加突出。例如，韦伯指出中国缺乏"严格保障的法律与理性的行政和司法"，这阻碍了资本主义的产生。[1]

分析宗教和其他因素在西方理性资本主义经济组织的独特发展

过程中的作用，似乎已经是一项庞大而复杂的计划，但韦伯并没有就此止步，他甚至更进一步开始研究西方文化中理性的兴起，其中包括资本主义经济、形态、理性法以及科层制 * 的产生。

至于《新教伦理与资本主义精神》如何与韦伯的整体研究联系起来，英国社会学家肯·莫里森指出："韦伯研究的缺点在于他并没有一个完整的体系和一个统一的主题"。[2] 事实上，德国社会学家弗里德里希·坦布鲁克等评论家也都认为，在韦伯的整个研究中很难找到一个统一的主题。[3]

意义

韦伯最负盛名和最有影响力的研究，是有关西方资本主义的产生及其独特的理性主义形式，《新教伦理与资本主义精神》是其代表作。* 许多学者对韦伯在《新教伦理与资本主义精神》中的观点持批评态度，却很少有人否认他在现代资本主义产生问题上的重要性，以及他的研究方法的独创性。

韦伯的《新教伦理与资本主义精神》是他首次尝试系统地解释现代资本主义社会的根源，也是他最著名的作品。肯·莫里森说"它一经发表就被视为经典之作"。[4] 这很大程度上是由于其观点的独创性，这部作品也奠定了韦伯作为社会学创始人之一的地位。正如社会学家凯兰·阿兰所说："《新教伦理与资本主义精神》被社会学家视为本学科的重要文本之一"。[5] 韦伯运用经验 * 方法进行缜密的历史研究，这种新兴的研究方法形成了今天的社会学研究范式。《新教伦理与资本主义精神》的出版和后来的翻译，使韦伯成为 20世纪最重要的思想家之一，至今仍享有盛誉。

1 马克斯·韦伯:《中国的宗教:儒教和道教》,汉斯·格斯译,纽约:自由出版社,1951年,第85页。

2 肯·莫里森:《马克思、迪尔克姆、韦伯:现代社会思想的奠基人》,伦敦:世哲出版社,2006年,第275页。

3 弗里德里希·坦布鲁克:《马克斯·韦伯研究的统一主题》,载《英国社会学杂志》总31期,1980年第3期,第316—351页。

4 肯·莫里森:《马克思、迪尔克姆、韦伯:现代社会思想的奠基人》,第275页。

5 凯兰·阿兰:《马克斯·韦伯评述》,普卢托出版社,2004年,第32页。

第三部分：学术影响

9 最初反响

要 点 ✐━

- 批评者指责韦伯忽视了资本主义＊形成中的其他原因，而过高估计了新教＊对产生"资本主义精神"＊的作用。
- 韦伯反驳说，他并没有试图全面解释资本主义的产生，并为新教教派＊与"资本主义精神"的关系极力争辩。
- 这部作品因其原创性而得到广泛的认同。

批评

历史学家卡尔·菲舍尔＊和菲利克斯·拉赫福尔＊，对马克斯·韦伯最初发表在期刊上的论文《新教伦理与资本主义精神》进行了详细的评论。德国经济学家路约·布伦塔诺＊和经济学家、社会学家维尔纳·桑巴特＊也在自己的书中对此展开批评，桑巴特还是发表韦伯论文的期刊的主编之一。

评论家称韦伯的研究太片面。有些人认为他没有完全解释资本主义的起源，另一些人认为他过于关注思想的作用而忽视其他可能的因素。桑巴特认为，犹太人已经成为资本主义的先锋："现在，如果清教主义＊对经济能产生影响，那么犹太教＊不是影响更大吗？没有哪种文明的宗教能像犹太教那样渗透进整个国家的生活。"[1] 布伦塔诺提出了更具体的批评。他认为，宗教改革＊前的好几个世纪里，信奉罗马天主教＊的意大利商人身上，就存在着"资本主义精神"之类的东西。＊布伦塔诺指出，"意大利商业城市威尼斯、热那亚和比萨在商业运作和贸易政策方面都非常资本主义……这都是在新教出现之前。"[2]但是韦伯没有注意到这一趋势。

菲舍尔对宗教与"资本主义精神"之间的关系提出质疑。他认为"资本主义精神和韦伯认为与之相关的责任观念都不一定是受到了宗教的影响"。[3]菲舍尔认为,韦伯没有充分考虑政治和社会力量产生"资本主义精神"的可能性。[4]经过宗教改革,思想观念已经随着经济环境的变化发生了改变。[5]菲舍尔认为这可能导致新教与资本主义发生了联系。

拉赫福尔也对韦伯的观点提出质疑,他认为"韦伯没有提供足够的证据来证实他自己的论点,因而未能正确地阐释新教与资本主义之间的关系"。[6]拉赫福尔提出,荷兰的资本主义出现在加尔文主义＊之前,当时的许多资本家都是罗马天主教徒。在清教徒扎根之前,英格兰也是如此。他认为,韦伯能够表明清教徒的商业活动具有宗教动机的证据不足。[7]

> 在某种程度上,围绕韦伯《新教伦理与资本主义精神》的争议从一开始就发生了。
>
> 《马克斯·韦伯传》

回应

韦伯在最初发表《新教伦理与资本主义精神》的期刊《社会科学与社会政治学文献》＊上,发表了一系列"反批评"来回应对他的批评。[8]他在1920年出版的《新教伦理与资本主义精神》一书中也作出了回应。

韦伯认为菲舍尔和拉赫福尔的批评无关紧要。因为完全解释资本主义的起源从来都不是他的目标，他只想探讨新教与现代资本主义之间的关系，此外他也从未怀疑过资本主义早在加尔文主义之前就存在了。他在全文和结论中都强调了自己的目标仅限于此。韦伯也承认，批评者们所提出的许多因素确实是有助于资本主义产生的。[9]

1920 年原论文出版成书，韦伯在增加的注释中回应了布伦塔诺的批评，即他忽略了中世纪和文艺复兴时期的罗马天主教私营业主。他坚持认为是新教徒，而不是他们的罗马天主教前辈，采用了资本主义经济伦理的方法，它产生的工作"强度"需要打破"经济传统主义"。*[10]

至于桑巴特提出的犹太人已经出现了资本主义的形式，韦伯认为，犹太民族的"局外人"地位并不意味着他们的社会影响力比清教徒小。[11] 在韦伯看来，犹太人接受这种局外人身份，因此他们可以保持"仪式的纯洁性"：只能"与局外人进行阴暗的经济交易"。[12] 犹太民族的局外人地位将他们排除在"与持续的、系统的和合理化的*工业企业相一致的经济活动"之外。[13]

韦伯运用语文学*（对语言的研究，包括文学批评、历史和语言学研究）批评菲舍尔没有为他的论点提供任何令人信服的证据："语文学研究显然可以在任何时候纠正我的结论。但是证据表明，仅仅反对是没有用的。"[14] 菲舍尔认为，韦伯应该考虑所有可能的因素，来证明宗教是决定经济行为的最重要因素。韦伯回应说这是不可能的，这只会让他走向反面。[15]

韦伯用同样的方法回应了拉赫福尔的批评。[16] 他重申自己的观点，即一个人的宗教职业会影响其生活方式。[17] 他还建议，批评者再读一下他关于资本主义产生有多种原因的原始观点。[18]

冲突与共识

　　韦伯在 1920 年出版的《新教伦理与资本主义精神》一书中，所做的大部分补充都是为了回应桑巴特和布伦塔诺的批评。比起拉赫福尔和菲舍尔，韦伯对他们的评论更加重视，但他仍然反驳了他们的批评。在 1920 年版的补充中，韦伯没有特意改变 1905 年论文中的基本要素，只是展开说明了观点。这证明，韦伯对他在《新教伦理与资本主义精神》中所提出的观点十分自信。

　　《新教伦理与资本主义精神》是 20 世纪最重要和最有影响力的作品之一。不出意料，它已经引起了无数学者的兴趣。有些学者仍在讨论关于新教作用于现代资本主义产生的"韦伯命题"是否成立。例如，意大利德裔经济学家达维德·坎托尼 * 表示反对。[19] 而加拿大经济学家伦纳德·达德利 * 和德国经济学家乌尔里希·布卢姆 * 则找出论据支持。[20]

　　总之，研究者把《新教伦理与资本主义精神》作为经典和研究的基础。问世一个多世纪以后的今天，还有少数韦伯研究者仍在讨论《新教伦理与资本主义精神》所提出的问题。

1　维尔纳·桑巴特：《犹太教与现代资本主义》，基奇纳，安大略：巴托什出版社，2001 年，第 134 页。

2　保罗·D. 谢弗：《革命与文艺复兴》，渥太华：渥太华大学出版社，2008 年，第 30 页。

3　斯蒂芬·特纳：《剑桥韦伯指南》，剑桥：剑桥大学出版社，2000 年，第 163—

164 页。

4　特纳：《剑桥韦伯指南》，第 164 页。

5　特纳：《剑桥韦伯指南》，第 164 页。

6　特纳：《剑桥韦伯指南》，第 164 页。

7　特纳：《剑桥韦伯指南》，第 164 页。

8　《社会科学与社会政治学文献》，由韦伯、维尔纳·桑巴特和埃德加·雅费创编，是当时德国的前沿学术期刊。

9　斯蒂芬·特纳：《剑桥韦伯指南》，剑桥：剑桥大学出版社，2000 年，第 162 页。

10　哈特穆特·莱曼、冈瑟·罗斯：《韦伯的新教伦理》，剑桥：剑桥大学出版社，1995 年，第 228 页。

11　莱曼、罗斯：《韦伯的新教伦理》，第 230 页。

12　莱曼、罗斯：《韦伯的新教伦理》，第 230—231 页。

13　莱曼、罗斯：《韦伯的新教伦理》，第 231 页。

14　山姆·惠姆斯特：《理解韦伯》，纽约：劳德里奇出版社，2007 年，第 119 页。

15　惠姆斯特：《理解韦伯》，纽约：劳德里奇出版社，2007 年，第 119 页。

16　惠姆斯特：《理解韦伯》，第 120 页。

17　惠姆斯特：《理解韦伯》，第 120 页。

18　马克斯·韦伯：《新教伦理与资本主义精神》，塔尔科特·帕森斯译，伦敦：劳德里奇出版社，2005 年，第 49 页。

19　达维德·坎托尼：《新教改革对经济的影响》，载《欧洲经济学会期刊》总 13 期，2014 年第 4 期，第 561—598 页。

20　乌尔里希·百隆、伦纳德达·德利：《宗教与经济增长》，载《进化经济学》总 11 期，2001 年第 2 期，第 207—230 页。

10 后续争议

要点 🔑

- 《新教伦理与资本主义精神》对人们如何思考资本主义*和现代社会的产生具有深远的影响。

- 在此基础上形成的思想流派，包括塔尔科特·帕森斯*的功能主义*理论和受马克思主义启发的冲突理论*。"功能主义"的理论方法，将社会视为一个由维持不同功能的各部分组成的整体。

- 《新教伦理与资本主义精神》是社会学*的奠基之作，仍影响着今天的学术研究。

应用与问题

马克斯·韦伯的《新教伦理与资本主义精神》出版以来，对它的解读已经发生了重大的变化。最初的争议主要集中在被称为"韦伯命题"的观点是否正确。争议仍在进行，社会学家又开始更多地关注韦伯研究的理论意义，并探讨如何将其应用到不同的分支领域。

1930 年，社会学家塔尔科特·帕森斯将此书翻译成英文，将它带到全球学术界，引起了更广泛的关注。20 世纪三四十年代，《新教伦理与资本主义精神》成为社会学领域的奠基之作。帕森斯翻译和解释此书的方式，使其更接近于法国社会学家埃米尔·迪尔克姆*的"功能主义"[1]（这一理论认为不同的社会行为都有其构成社会的有用"目的"）。但这种解释也使韦伯成为卡尔·马克思*的对立面，低估了物质利益和冲突在资本主义产生中的作用。[2]

20世纪七八十年代，三位最重要的当代社会学理论家——法国的皮埃尔·布尔迪厄*、英国的安东尼·吉登斯*和德国的尤尔根·哈贝马斯*，分别在他们的"实践""结构化"*和"交往行动"*理论中继承发展了马克思、韦伯和迪尔克姆的思想。[3] 除了借鉴韦伯的统治类型和冲突思想，他们还借用了《新教伦理与资本主义精神》的新观点。他们分析了现代资本主义形成的"生活方式"，重新使用韦伯的一些经典概念，诸如"世界的祛魅"*（神圣性无法与西方社会日益增长的理性特征共存）。

今天，大部分关于《新教伦理与资本主义精神》的争议，已不再集中于它与宏观社会学理论的关系，而在于它在社会学不同分支领域的应用。只有专门研究韦伯和《新教伦理与资本主义精神》的学者还在进一步讨论，比如英国历史学家彼得·戈什*和瑞典社会学家理查德·斯威德伯格。*

> 资本主义的本质就是追求利润，并通过持续的、理性的资本主义生产方式不断地获利。
>
> 马克斯·韦伯：《新教伦理与资本主义精神》

思想流派

马克斯·韦伯把《新教伦理与资本主义精神》视为对马克思主义*经济学家维尔纳·桑巴特*1902年出版的著作《现代资本主义》的一种回应。研究者们一般认为，其内容至少有一部分，是对马克思主义唯物史观的批判。*但是从20世纪50年代后期开始，特别是在20世纪六七十年代，马克思主义风格的社会学家开始受其影响。他们的"冲突理论"连接了马克思和韦伯，成为塔尔科特·帕森斯功能主义倾向的对立面。

有些学者侧重于韦伯提出的冲突、利益、统治、科层制、合理性，而不是强调与其价值观一致。比如美国社会学家莱特·米尔斯*、艾文·古尔德纳*以及德国英裔社会学家拉尔夫·达伦多夫*等。米尔斯的《白领：美国中产阶级》[4] 发展了韦伯关于科层化（政府或企业的行政管理特征日益增强）进程的论点。在《工业组织的科层制类型》中，[5] 艾文·古尔德纳（马克思主义社会学家）讨论了官僚主义在多大程度上可以用来支配个人。韦伯还启发了许多可以被称为"纯韦伯式"的学者，他们并不整合韦伯与其他重要学者的理论，而是单纯从其原始背景和目的出发对韦伯作品进行研究和解释，并运用他的思想来帮助我们理解其他时期和地区的问题。德国和英国学者在这方面最为突出，其中赖因哈德·本迪克斯*和布莱恩·特纳*最具影响力。

社会学各分支领域的不同流派也都运用了《新教伦理与资本主义精神》的思想。例如，在经济社会学*（研究经济行为在社会中的嵌入方式）领域，瑞典社会学家理查德·斯维德伯格*研究不合理性*的行为、符合价值理性*的行为和传统的经济行为（"价值理性"是指为了其固有的价值而不是为了实现特定目标而采取的行动），具有很大的影响力。[6]

当代研究

受韦伯启发的学者不断作出新的贡献，尤其是在社会学理论、政治学和经济社会学领域。例如，著名印度人类学家*阿尔让·阿帕杜莱*受韦伯"资本主义精神"启发，提出了计算的"精神"。

韦伯的许多追随者，如德国社会学家沃尔夫冈·施罗特*，发现韦伯的主要贡献在于他对西方理性化的理解——理性思维在社会生活中日益占主导地位的过程。这个过程发生在宗教、工作、会计、政治和法律中，尽管并不总是相互关联。尤尔根·哈贝马斯认为，韦伯对现代社会的诊断是理解理性、正当的决策行为的社会学基础。他指的不仅是哲学理想，还包括实际的可能性。换句话说，哈贝马斯著名的协商民主*政治理论的社会学基础（一种以讨论和反思为基础的决策制定的民主形式），很大程度上要归功于韦伯。[7]

另一位关注现代化并受韦伯启发的学者，是美国政治学家罗纳德·英格尔哈特。*韦伯指出，随着各国资本主义的发展，人们的价值观会发生变化。当经济的资本主义化加深，人们的传统价值观就会转向更追求经济和物质保障的现代物质主义*价值观。英格尔哈特进一步指出，当经济不断发展，人们的价值观就更关注自我表达和生活质量。[8]与之不同的是，法国社会学家吕克·博尔坦斯基*与伊芙·夏佩罗*指出，资本主义仍然需要一种精神。他们认为，在现代社会中大部分人并没有在宗教中寻找这种精神。相反，人们可能会在深受管理思想影响的管理层和执行层中找到它。[9]

理查德·斯维德伯格在经济社会学领域开创了韦伯式的研究，他的目标是提出一种关注理性决策和网络的替代方案。斯维德伯格使得经济社会学开始关注价值观和传统在经济行为中的作用。而其他学者对这些问题还只有一些假设。斯威德伯格还认为，皮埃尔·布尔迪厄对经济社会学的重要贡献也是来自韦伯的启发。他认为，布尔迪厄用"世界的祛魅"来理解阿尔及利亚农民，应归功于韦伯的《新教伦理与资本主义精神》。[10]

1 米歇尔·狄龙:《社会学理论概论》,奇切斯特:约翰·威立父子出版社,2009年,第156页。

2 肯·莫里森:《马克思、迪尔克姆、韦伯:现代社会思想的奠基人》,伦敦:世哲出版社,2006年,第295页。

3 保罗·兰塞姆:《社会理论入门》,布里斯托尔:政治出版社,2010年,第291页。

4 C·莱特·米尔斯:《白领:美国的中产阶级》,牛津:牛津大学出版社,2002年。

5 阿尔文·古尔德纳:《工业组织的科层制类型》,自由出版社,1964年。

6 理查德·斯威德伯格:《马克斯·韦伯与经济社会学思想》,纽约普林斯顿:普林斯顿大学出版社,2000年。

7 约翰·麦克密克:《韦伯、哈贝马斯和欧洲国家的转变》,剑桥:剑桥大学出版社,2007年。

8 罗纳德·英格尔哈特:《现代化与后现代化文化:43个国家的文化、经济和政治变迁》,纽约普林斯顿:普林斯顿大学出版社,1997年。

9 卢克·布尔当斯基、伊芙·夏佩罗:《新资本主义精神》,载《国际政治、文化、社会杂志》总18期,2005年第3—4期,第161—188页。

10 理查德·斯威德伯格:《皮埃尔·布尔迪厄的经济社会学理论》,载《文化社会学》总5期,2011第1期,第69页。

11 当代印迹

要点 ⚿

- 多数学者认为，《新教伦理与资本主义精神》至今仍是一部经典著作，是社会学*的奠基之作。
- 《新教伦理与资本主义精神》发表一个多世纪后，仍在引发有关现代资本主义*社会源起的争议。
- 虽然有些学者还在继续讨论韦伯的论点，但今天的学术研究大都是将韦伯的思想应用于新的学科领域。

地位

正如英国社会学家彼得·汉密尔顿指出的，马克斯·韦伯的《新教伦理与资本主义精神》是一部不朽名著。[1] 韦伯写道："现代经济社会中人们的宗教根源已经死亡；在今天的世界里，天职的概念就是一个残躯。"[2] 这个字面翻译为"死头"的拉丁短语，是指"无用的残余"。由于这构成了韦伯的主要论点，人们可能会认为《新教伦理与资本主义精神》对今天的意义有限。毕竟，韦伯研究的是资本主义的产生，他并不关心一百年后我们这个时代的制度状况。

然而，《新教伦理与资本主义精神》对今天仍有启示，不是因为它的主要论点，而是因为它激发了一种更为普遍的思考社会变革的方式。美国政治学家弗朗西斯·福山*认为，虽然经济学家并没有特别重视韦伯的经济增长文化理论，但他们仍然注意到他关于宗教和文化在制度成效中的作用的观点。[3] 这一观点可以帮助解释当代的问题。例如，新教徒 * 和罗马天主教 * 国家对腐败的不同态度。⁴ 福山还指出，《新教伦理与资本主义精神》已经提出了"关于宗教在现代生活中的作用的深刻问题。"[5]

此外，韦伯对西方社会理性化 * 的描述似乎一直是准确的。如他所见，我们已经看到"基于理性科学的资本主义已遍布全球，将物质进步带到了世界上大部分地区，并将其统统桎梏于我们现在称之为全球化的铁笼 * 之中。"[6] 如果说《新教伦理与资本主义精神》激起了新的论争，那未免有些夸张，但它的观点显然仍可运用于当代有关宗教与经济行为之间关系的争议。福山认为，"印度教 * 在印度中产阶级中的复兴……美国宗教的持续活跃，都表明世俗化 * 和理性主义 * 并不是现代化的必然手段。"[7] 这个过程并不完全符合韦伯在《新教伦理与资本主义精神》中的观点，但它确实说明了韦伯研究经久不衰的意义。

《新教伦理与资本主义精神》受到如此广泛的关注，要对其观点形成共识几乎是不可能的。正如社会学家布莱恩·特纳 * 所说，"新教伦理是一个永远讨论不完的命题"。[8] 无论如何，韦伯的《新教伦理与资本主义精神》毫无疑问仍是一部经典之作。

> 当今时代的特征就是韦伯式的。
>
> 阿拉斯戴尔·麦金泰尔：《追寻美德》

互动

正如英国社会学家安东尼·吉登斯 * 所说，《新教伦理与资本主义精神》是"极具争议的……并且是针对经济决定论 * 的"。在吉登斯看来，"很明显韦伯针对的是马克思主义，至少是针对其最为突出的简单粗暴的历史分析方法"。⁹ 韦伯关于宗教观念如何决定一个社会经济发展的论点，向同时代的马克思主义经济学家和政治理论家提出了挑战。韦伯证明了思想也具有影响历史的重要力量，由此打破了物质条件决定社会经济和阶级结构的观点。因此，只有那些接受马克思主义的当代思想家才与其前辈一样，仍然受到韦伯《新教伦理与资本主义精神》的挑战。

尽管《新教伦理与资本主义精神》仍在引发争议，学者们继续向韦伯命题发起挑战，但这些挑战并非来自理论和意识形态的冲突。相反，研究者希望证明"韦伯命题"——20 世纪最具争议的论点——是否仍然适用。例如，达维德·坎托尼 * 对韦伯命题持否定意见，¹⁰ 而伦纳德·达德利 * 和乌尔里希·布卢姆 * 则表示支持。¹¹

持续争议

今天，关于《新教伦理与资本主义精神》的大多数讨论都不在大的社会学理论上，而是将其应用于社会学的分支领域。只有一小群特定的韦伯研究者仍在讨论其原始内容和意义，¹² 大部分学者都是将它作为相关领域新兴研究的起点。

尽管如此，对这部著作内容的讨论还在继续；其中最著名的议题大概是韦伯命题如何解释西方理性化 * 和资本主义的产生。¹³ 研究比较政治学和政治文化的当代学者，如罗纳德·英格尔哈特 * 和英美政治社会学家皮帕·诺里斯 *，对韦伯关于社会的理性化加剧其世俗化 * 的论点进行了高度评价。¹⁴

社会学不断重新审视其创始人的关注点和方法，而韦伯始终是最有影响力的社会学家之一。《新教伦理与资本主义精神》1920 年版在 2001 年重新翻译成英译本，这个新版本规范了韦伯的术语，恢复了原来的斜体字，体现了韦伯论点的细微差别。[15]《经典社会学》期刊经常发表有关韦伯的研究论文，《马克斯·韦伯研究》也是专门讨论韦伯研究的期刊。这些研究论文经常涉及《新教伦理与资本主义精神》的关键主题。

1　彼得·汉密尔顿主编：《马克斯·韦伯简评》第 1 卷，伦敦：劳德里奇出版社，1991 年，第 308 页。

2　彼得·汉密尔顿主编：《马克斯·韦伯简评》，第 308 页。

3　弗朗西斯·福山：《加尔文主义宣言》，载《纽约时报》2005 年 3 月 13 日，登录日期 2015 年 10 月 18 日，http://www.nytimes.com/2005/03/13/books/review/the-calvinist-manifesto.html

4　弗朗西斯·福山：《加尔文主义宣言》

5　弗朗西斯·福山：《加尔文主义宣言》

6　弗朗西斯·福山：《加尔文主义宣言》

7　弗朗西斯·福山：《加尔文主义宣言》

8　布莱恩·特纳、马克斯·韦伯：《从历史到现代》，纽约：劳德里奇出版社，2002 年，第 25 页。

9　马克斯·韦伯：《新教伦理与资本主义精神》，伦敦和纽约：劳德里奇出版社，第 XVII 页。

10　达维德·坎托尼：《新教改革对经济的影响》，载《欧洲经济学会期刊》总 13 期，2014 年第 4 期，第 561—598 页。

11　乌尔里希·百隆、伦纳德达·德利：《宗教与经济增长》，载《进化经济学》总 11 期，2001 年第 2 期，第 207—230 页。

12　理查德·斯威德伯格，《马克斯·韦伯与经济社会学思想》，纽约普林斯顿：普林斯顿大学出版社，2000 年；彼得·戈什，《马克斯·韦伯与新教伦理》，牛津：

牛津大学出版社，2014 年。

13 尼古拉斯·甘恩:《马克斯·韦伯与后现代理论》，贝辛斯托克：帕尔格雷夫，2002 年。

14 皮帕·诺里斯、罗纳德·英格尔哈特:《神圣与世俗》，剑桥：剑桥大学出版社，2011 年。

15 马克斯·韦伯:《新教伦理与资本主义精神》，斯蒂芬·卡尔伯格译，第 4 版，纽约：牛津大学出版社，2009 年。

12 未来展望

要点 🔑

- 《新教伦理与资本主义精神》在未来的许多年里可能仍是一部杰作。

- 随着资本主义 * 的不断发展，《新教伦理与资本主义精神》关于西方资本主义产生和理性化 * 进程的论点，仍然具有现实意义。

- 《新教伦理与资本主义精神》奠定了社会学 * 学科的基础。

潜力

马克斯·韦伯的《新教伦理与资本主义精神》可能在未来的很长一段时间内都仍是经典。社会学家已经讨论了一百多年了，目前似乎还不太可能改变。[1] 因为《新教伦理与资本主义精神》，韦伯也仍然会是社会学学科的重要人物。一般社会理论各分支学科的学者们也一直在讨论韦伯，他们的讨论依然很强劲，虽然这些学科的发展较之其他领域还显缓慢。但是，在许多不断发展的分支领域，如经济社会学 *（研究经济学融入社会行为的方式）和文化社会学 *（研究塑造文化的社会结构和符号），研究者们仍在引用《新教伦理与资本主义精神》。

许多当代社会学家发现，自己提出的问题与韦伯在一个世纪前所讨论的十分相似。早期社会学家提出的许多解释，今天也仍然具有现实意义。这种持续的关切将社会学与其他社会科学区分开来，也使这一学科创始人的重要性更加显著。换句话说，社会学家并不一定将《新教伦理与资本主义精神》视为一种准确的经验 * 研究方法。相反，他们是被其原创性力量所吸引：它所提出的问题以及它激发学者提出的假设。今天，韦伯的论著常常成为相关研究的催化剂，它可以引发关于文化价值观在经济发展中作用的研究，可以用来进行不同社会的跨文化比较，也可以帮助开展围绕现代性和理性发展的讨论。

> 社会学……是一门对社会行为进行解释性理解，从而对其过程和结果进行因果解释的科学。
>
> 马克斯·韦伯：《经济与社会》

未来方向

作为社会学学科的基础性研究，《新教伦理与资本主义精神》已经产生了无法估量的学术价值。在其出版后的一个多世纪里，学者们几乎穷尽了研究的所有可能。韦伯认为历史没有"铁律"，[2] "社会理论的任务"是帮助人们"寻找历史的真相"。[3] 韦伯不同意马克思主义认为学术研究应该改变社会的观点。[4] 因此，韦伯式的学者不会去认定任何具体事实。相反，他们希望通过公正合理的研究来发现事实。如果说韦伯引领了一批追随者，那么他会希望他们成为有能力追求自己学问的研究者。因此，我们很难确定哪些学者是韦伯的继承者。

此外，不同时代的学者对韦伯的所有实质性论点都提出了极大的疑问。的确，美国政治学家弗朗西斯·福山＊等有影响力的思想家认为，韦伯关于宗教和文化对经济行为产生影响的论点长期具有重要意义。[5] 英国社会学家安东尼·吉登斯＊则指出，我们可能会质疑韦伯所有论点的细节："我不认为韦伯的个人主义方法论经得起时间的考验……其科层制*理论显然已经过时了……当然，也无法证明如韦伯所说的，新教*或清教主义*是现代资本主义的起源。"6

针对韦伯论点提出的各种疑问，很少有学者愿意进一步开展研究。

小结

马克斯·韦伯在《新教伦理与资本主义精神》中指出，追求利润的严谨的生活方式是现代资本主义产生的重要力量。他相信是新教神学*激发了追求利润的动机。这一观点自发表以来就引起了广泛的关注，被称为"韦伯命题"。《新教伦理与资本主义精神》并不是鸿篇巨制，却解决了当代社会学作为一门学科创立的重要问题。不同思想流派的韦伯追随者们，都将这一命题长期视为社会学的基本问题和研究路径。例如，对现代资本主义和西方理性主义*的起源和未来发展的研究，以及对信仰、价值观、传统和非物质利益的研究兴趣，都可以追溯到韦伯。

韦伯认为宗教观念可能引起经济变革。这使他早早地与马克思主义哲学强有力的"唯物主义"*观点分道扬镳。有一段时间，学者们认为这是韦伯原创性的核心。但是今天许多学者试图将韦伯和卡尔·马克思*的观点整合起来，认为马克思并没有那么强调唯物主义，而韦伯也并没有那么强调思想的作用。此外，原著还包含着一些晦涩的内容，特别是关于"选择性亲和力"*等关键概念。部分原因可能是因为最初发表的论文和最终出版的论著之间相隔15年，其间韦伯作了一些重要的补充。无论如何，韦伯为后世的解读留下了空间，多年来引发了无数争议。

  《新教伦理与资本主义精神》激发了许多新的研究假设。甚至只是其中的一些不太重要的概念——比如"世界的祛魅"*"铁笼"*，都已经独立发展成为经典的社会学概念。韦伯的其他作品也逐渐被视为经典。几十年来，社会学家几乎一致认为他是该学科的三大创始人之一，另外两位是卡尔·马克思*和埃米尔·迪尔克姆*。

  正如社会学创始人的其他名著一样，《新教伦理与资本主义精神》的价值也不会随着时间的推移而消减。当代社会学的研究和理论有许多是来自这部作品提出的问题，以及伟大的思想家们围绕它展开的讨论。实际上，正是这些讨论在很大程度上造就了社会学这门学科。每一个对社会学感兴趣的人都会在韦伯的研究中获得灵感，尤其是《新教伦理与资本主义精神》。

---

1 凯兰·阿兰：《马克斯·韦伯评述》，普卢托出版社，2004年，第32页。

2 冈瑟·罗斯、沃尔夫冈·施罗特：《马克斯·韦伯的历史观》，加州伯克利：加利福尼亚大学出版社，1984年，第201页。

3 肯·莫里森：《马克思、迪尔克姆、韦伯：现代社会思想的奠基人》，伦敦：世哲出版社，2006年，第276页。

4 肯·莫里森：《马克思、迪尔克姆、韦伯：现代社会思想的奠基人》，伦敦：世哲出版社，2006年，第276页。

5 弗朗西斯·福山：《加尔文主义宣言》，载《纽约时报》2005年3月13日，登录日期2015年10月18日，http://www.nytimes.com/2005/03/13/books/review/the-calvinist-manifesto.html.

6 安东尼·吉登斯、克里斯托弗·皮尔森：《与吉登斯对话：理解现代性》，加州斯坦福：斯坦福大学出版社，1998年，第60—61页。

术语表

1. **古罗马**：最大、最重要的文明古国之一，兴起于公元前 8 世纪，延续至公元 5 世纪。

2. **人类学**：研究人的学科。主要进行不同文化的比较研究，观察不同社会结构的演变。

3. **《社会科学与社会政治学文献》**：当时领先的德国学术刊物，由韦伯、维尔纳·桑巴特和埃德加·雅费主编。

4. **禁欲主义**：韦伯定义为对欢愉的自我否定。他认为，在现代资本主义中，自我控制和克己成为一种社会行为，它创造了一种严谨的工作方式。禁欲主义源自宗教，但韦伯认为，到了 19 世纪，禁欲主义已经成为日常生活的一部分。

5. **浸礼会**：新教宗派的一个分支，主张只对信徒施洗。因此他们反对给婴儿施洗的常规办法，认为洗礼必须让受洗人全身浸入水中。

6. **佛教**：一个关注个人灵修的宗教。佛教徒不相信造物主和上帝，而相信人们必须追随佛陀的道路，才能获得超脱，达到涅槃。全世界目前有近 4 亿佛教徒。

7. **科层制**：韦伯定义为伴随合理化过程的某种特定类型的行政结构。例如，科层制建立的等级结构是基于成员的功绩而不是其社会关系。

8. **天职观**："天职观"把个人工作视为上帝赋予的任务。这是 16 世纪德国神学家马丁·路德提出的概念。

9. **加尔文主义**：法国著名的宗教改革家、神学家约翰·加尔文的新教分支学说。加尔文主义强调上帝对万物的统治，其早期还宣扬预定论（哪些人能得救赎是上帝预先定下的，与他们现世的一切无关）。

10. **资本主义**：韦伯认为，在大部分社会中，人们在交易之初和之后开始计算预期利益，那么"资本主义"作为一种经济和社会制度就出

现了，所不同的只是交易的方式。"现代资本主义"或"西方资本主义"，则是在西欧和美国出现的一种更具体的经济组织。在现代资本主义中，自由劳动力以一种理性计算的方式组织起来，而"资本主义精神"引导社会有系统地追逐利润。对资本主义更通俗的理解，是指资本属于个人、生产资料不归集体所有的经济制度。

11. **普通法**：一种依据判例而不是法规的法律制度。个案中的判决作为法律的判例，这意味着过去的判例对未来的判决具有约束力。

12. **交往行动**：德国哲学家尤尔根·哈贝马斯定义为，人们之间进行协商和讨论的行动。

13. **儒家**：一种基于孔子思想的学说。孔子是生活在公元前5—6世纪的中国哲学家。

14. **文化社会学**：一门研究构成"文化"的社会行为和符号的学科。

15. **文化决定论**：一种强调文化在决定社会行为中的重要性的主张。

16. **协商民主**：一种以公共审议作为合法决策基础的民主形式。

17. **侨民**：一群离乡背井的人。它通常指被迫离开家园的人，但也可指自愿移民。

18. **世界的祛魅**：韦伯定义为在调解人类与世界的关系中，神圣性的作用逐渐消解的过程。新教（特别是加尔文宗）否认罗马天主教教廷可以救赎灵魂，这在祛魅中发挥了重要作用。

19. **经济决定论**：经济关系是解释一切社会现象的基础。这种观念与卡尔·马克思的学说密切相关。

20. *经济社会学*：一门研究经济制度和经济行为的社会原因的学科。这一术语最早出现在19世纪末，《新教伦理与资本主义精神》被认为是经济社会学最重要的著作之一。

21. *经济传统主义*：一种文化或经济伦理，认为工作是出于被迫，不如休闲更有价值，工作只是为了满足"传统需要"。

22. **选择性亲和力 / 内在亲和力**：这一有些含糊的术语多次出现在韦伯的著作中，并引起了一些争论。它是指两个具有共同特征或历史联系的现象之间的关系，但又无法清楚地证明其具有因果关系。因此，新教信仰并没有"产生"资本主义精神，但两者高度兼容。

23. **经验**：通过观察和实验获得的知识。人们通过感官来收集经验知识。

24. **认识论**：一个关于知识研究的哲学分支。

25. **欧洲中心主义**：从纯粹的欧洲视角看世界，认为欧洲文化优于其他文化。

26. **欧元区**：所有使用欧元作为货币的国家总称，包括德国、法国、西班牙等国。

27. **封建主义**：中世纪建立在领主和封臣关系基础上的政治经济体系。

28. **功能主义**：受生物学的启发，功能主义理论把社会看作一个整体，不同的组成部分对维持社会整体发挥着不同的功能。这一概念最早来自于法国哲学家奥古斯特·孔德和英国哲学家赫伯特·斯宾塞，埃米尔·迪尔克姆成为第一个采用功能主义的社会学家。韦伯的英文译者塔尔科特·帕森斯和他的追随者美国社会学家罗伯特·默顿进一步发展了这一理论，使之成为 20 世纪四五十年代的主流理论。

29. **适应性论文或教授资格论文**：获取教授资格所需的论文，是欧洲和亚洲某些国家取得博士学位后继续进行研究的最高学术论文。

30. **海德堡大学**：建立于 1386 年，是德国最古老的大学，以其独立思想和民主价值观而著称。

31. **印度教**：一个信徒超过 9 亿的世界性宗教，主要分布在印度和尼泊尔。它的历史可以追溯到几千年前，是世界上最古老的宗教之一。

32. **历史唯物主义**：卡尔·马克思的唯物史观指出，是经济基础决定上层建筑，而不是相反。

33. **人文学科**：研究人类文化的学科，包括历史、文学和哲学。

34. **理想主义**：这种哲学观点认为现实是一种心理现象，因此，必须通过对社会价值的解释来理解人类行为，而不能将其简化为物质利益。

35. **工业革命**：通过采用新的生产方式完成的经济转型，开始于 18 世纪中叶的英国，此后一百年里传播到了西欧。

36. **诠释社会学或理解社会学**：一种由韦伯和格奥尔格·西梅尔发展出的社会学理论，它不是侧重于描述事实，而是侧重于通过理解其主观意义来解释行为的原因和结果。

37. **铁笼**：韦伯将人类无法控制的物欲追求比喻为"钢铁般坚硬的外壳"。《新教伦理与资本主义精神》的第一位英文译者塔尔科特·帕森斯把它翻译为"铁笼"，这一比喻已成为韦伯理论的经典概念。

38. **犹太教**：最古老的世界宗教之一，其历史可以追溯到 3 500 年前。犹太人称自己是上帝的选民，应努力过一种神圣而有道德的生活。

39. **路德宗**：以马丁·路德宗教思想为依据的新教宗派，其教义核心是因信称义。

40. **循道宗**：18 世纪兴起的改革英格兰教会的宗教运动，到 18 世纪末已成为一个独立的教派。

41. **中世纪**：欧洲历史上的 5 世纪到 15 世纪，被认为是历史的中间阶段，处于古代和现代之前。

42. **新康德主义**：一个深受 18 世纪德国哲学家伊曼纽尔·康德思想影响的哲学流派，从 19 世纪 70 年代到第一次世界大战在德国处于主流地位。

43. **虔敬主义**：17 世纪发生在路德宗内部的一次变革，强调个人信仰高于一切。

44. **语文学**：研究语言和文本的学科，是一门包含文学批评、历史和语言学的综合学科。

45. **实证主义**：由 19 世纪法国哲学家奥古斯特·孔德提出的哲学思想，

他也是"社会学"一词的创始人。实证主义认为，获取知识的唯一有效途径是通过经验感知。"社会学之父"埃米尔·迪尔克姆进一步发展了实证主义的影响力。

46. **预定论**：一种相信命运由上帝预先决定、个人无能为力的观点。也指成事在天。

47. **前现代**：15世纪之前的历史时期，一般认为这一时期的社会生活由传统和宗教主宰。

48. **自由派神学**：一种普遍使用于各个基督教教派的神学思潮，主张基督教信仰与社会正义等进步思想的发展相适应。

49. **新教**：基督教的一大流派，宗教改革之后新教出现并与罗马天主教分裂。

50. **普鲁士**：1525—1947年间，位于今天德国和波兰部分地区的一个历史上的国家。

51. **清教主义**：韦伯的清教主义是指对欢愉的自我否定，并与世俗保持距离。加尔文宗等新教教派鼓励这种行为。清教主义旨在消除罗马天主教对新教信仰的影响。

52. **贵格会**：17世纪中期兴起的宗教团体"教友派"，强调每个成员都要按照上帝的旨意生活。

53. **理性计算**：韦伯是指在交易发生前后估算利润和损失的过程。

54. **理性（主义）**：韦伯的理性可用于指社会类型，也可指行为方式。理性社会是指普遍采用合理的规则标准与理性的计算方法的社会形态，理性行为是指为达到目的而精准计算的行为方式。

55. **理性化**：韦伯社会发展思想的重要概念，是指理性计算和理性行为导致社会生活越来越合理化的过程。

56. **宗教改革**：一场兴起于16世纪的改革罗马天主教会的宗教运动。这场宗教改革由德国神学家马丁·路德和法国神学家约翰·加尔文领导，各种新教教派随之在西欧出现。

57. **罗马天主教**：一个具有 2 000 年历史的传统基督教流派，也是最大的基督教教会，全世界信徒超过 12 亿。

58. **教派**：即宗教团体。与教会不同，他们只吸纳符合某些标准的成员，成员必须接受教派对其个人品行的监督。

59. **世俗**：即宗教组织和宗教信仰以外的世界。例如，世俗教育不接受宗教思想的指导，也不在宗教组织开展。

60. **社会学**：一门研究人类行为的学科，研究对象从个人行为到整体社会行为。社会学试图考察和解释人类社会行为的起源、组织方式，以及在不同社会体系中的发展变化。

61. **组织社会学**：对正式组织和非正式组织的社会学研究，侧重研究组织如何决定人们的行为方式。

62. **"资本主义精神"**：韦伯用来指称以金钱、利润、工作、竞争和物质成功为终极目标的生活体系。按照韦伯的说法，"资本主义精神"来源于加尔文学说的救赎思想，加尔文强调个人自律，并将这一要求扩展到个人的经济行为中去。

63. **结构化理论**：社会学家安东尼·吉登斯提出的理论，认为社会生活不仅仅是个人行为的总和，也不仅仅取决于社会力量。由于人们和社会结构之间存在互动，传统等社会结构也会随之而改变。

64. **道家**：一种中国的传统哲学和宗教信仰。道家思想以"道"为最高信仰，也被翻译为"大道"。"道"的实质很难定义，可以理解为宇宙创世理论。

65. **神学**：即对宗教思想的研究，也可作为特定宗教思想和观念的总称，如：新教神学。

66. **上帝一位论**：一种认为上帝是唯一存在的神学观点，反对通常理解的上帝是圣父、圣子、圣灵三位一体的学说。

67. **弗赖堡大学**：建立于 1457 年，是德国第五古老的大学，有着教授社会科学和自然科学的悠久传统。

68. **功利主义**：一种以实际功效或利益作为道德标准的伦理学说。为了追求幸福，人们依据能否提高最大快乐值、降低最小痛苦值作为善恶标准。

69. **社会政策联盟**：由德国经济学家创立于 1873 年的一个具有影响力的社会团体，其成员包括马克斯·韦伯和维尔纳·桑巴特。

70. **天职**：一种将职业视为"神召"或上帝赋予使命的工作伦理。韦伯研究了多种宗教信仰，但只在新教中发现这种伦理。

71. **第一次世界大战**：1914 年至 1918 年间以欧洲为中心的一场世界大战，法国、英国、俄罗斯和美国为一方，德国、奥匈帝国和奥斯曼帝国为另一方。

人名表

1. 阿尔让·阿帕杜莱（1949 年生），美国印裔人类学家，现代性和全球化研究领域最具影响力的当代学者之一。代表作为《消散的现代性：全球化的文化维度》（1996），书中大量引用了韦伯的观点。

2. 萨沙·贝克尔（1973 年生），德国经济学家，目前在华威大学工作。研究方向为经济史和劳动经济学。

3. 赖因哈德·本迪克斯（1916—1991），移民美国的德国社会学家，代表作为《马克斯·韦伯思想肖像》（1960）。

4. 詹姆斯·布劳特（1927—2000），伊利诺伊大学的人类学和地理学教授，欧洲中心主义的最重要批评者之一。

5. 乌尔里希·布卢姆（1953 年生），德国马丁路德哈勒-维滕贝格德大学经济学家，研究方向为制度经济学和工业经济学。

6. 吕克·博尔坦斯基（1940 年生），法国"实用主义社会学"的领军人物，代表作为与夏娃·希亚佩洛合著的《资本主义的新精神》（1999）。

7. 皮埃尔·布尔迪厄（1930—2002），法国著名社会学家、哲学家，代表作为《区隔：审美品位的社会批判》和《实践理论概要》（1977）。这两部作品均由理查德·尼斯译成英文版。

8. 路约·布伦塔诺（1844—1931），与韦伯同时代的德国经济学家，他的著作《现代资本主义的兴起》（1916）对韦伯产生了很大的影响。

9. 约翰·加尔文（1509—1564），法国著名宗教改革家、神学家，新教加尔文教派的创始人，主张因信称义，谁能得救是上帝预定的。

10. 达维德·坎托尼（1981 年生），德国慕尼黑路德维希马克西米利安大学的意裔经济学家，研究方向为经济史和政治经济学。

11. 夏娃·希亚佩洛（1965 年生），法国管理学教授，代表作为合著的《资本主义的新精神》（1999）。

12. 拉尔夫·达伦多夫（1929—2009），德国英裔社会学家、政治家，在其代表作《工业社会中的阶级和阶级冲突》（1957）中提出的冲突理论最具影响力。

13. 威廉·狄尔泰（1833—1911），德国哲学家，代表作为《精神科学导论》（1923）。

14. 伦纳德·达德利（1943年生），加拿大蒙特利尔大学经济学家，研究方向为信息技术对经济增长和政治制度的影响。

15. 埃米尔·迪尔克姆（1858—1917），法国社会学家，代表作为《宗教生活的基本形式》（1912）、《自杀论》（1897）和《社会分工论》（1893）。

16. 卡尔·菲舍尔，生平不详，韦伯时代曾活跃在德国学术界，除了与韦伯的论辩外没有其他著述，他可能是生于1840年的德国历史学家。

17. 本杰明·富兰克林（1706—1790），美国开国元勋之一，也是政治家、科学家、出版商、外交官、发明家和作家。

18 弗朗西斯·福山（1952年生），美国政治学家和理论家，代表作为《历史的终结和最后的人》（1992）。他提出，在苏联解体后，自由资本主义已成为人类政治的最终形式。

19. 彼得·戈什，英国牛津大学历史学家，研究方向为19世纪英国政治与政治思想，以及马克斯·韦伯研究。

20. 安东尼·吉登斯（1938年生），英国著名社会学家，代表作为《社会的构成》（1984）。吉登斯被公认为是最重要的社会学家之一——如果不是最重要的话，他在人文学科高被引学者中名列第五。

21. 埃伯哈德·哥赛因（1853—1923），文化和经济史学家，他坚定地支持德国社会学会的创立，其代表作为《黑森林经济史》（1892）。

22. 艾文·古尔德纳（1920—1980），美国著名的马克思主义社会学家，代表作为《西方社会学面临的危机》（1970）和《工业官僚体制的模式》（1954），后者将韦伯的概念应用于产业关系的研究。

23. 尤尔根·哈贝马斯（1929年生），德国著名社会学家和哲学家，代表作为《交往行为理论》（1981），其中一节专门论述了《新教伦理与资本主义精神》。

24. **罗纳德·英格尔哈特**（1934年生），美国著名政治学家，代表作为《现代化与后现代化：43个国家的文化、经济与政治变迁》（1997）。

25. **埃德加·雅费**（1861—1921），马克斯·韦伯和维尔纳·桑巴特的学生，也是《社会学和社会政治学文献》的编辑，研究方向为英国经济。

26. **格奥尔格·耶利内克**（1851—1911），奥地利法学家、法哲学家，代表作为《人权和公民权宣言》（1895），致力于研究清教运动的社会影响。

27. **马丁·路德**（1483—1546），德国神学家、宗教改革倡导者，他认为人们应该用自己的语言阅读《圣经》，1534年出版了德译版《圣经》。路德宗是根据马丁·路德神学思想创立的基督教新教宗派。

28. **卡尔·马克思**（1818—1883），德国哲学家、记者、经济学家、社会学家和革命家，代表作为《共产党宣言》（与弗里德里希·恩格斯共同起草，1848）和《资本论》（1867—1894）。

29. **查尔斯·赖特·米尔斯**（1916—1962），20世纪中叶美国最具影响力的社会学家之一，代表作为《权力精英》（1956）和《社会学的想象力》（1959），与社会学家格斯合译的《韦伯社会学文选》（1948）则将韦伯引入了英语世界。

30. **皮帕·诺里斯**（1953年生），政治学家，哈佛大学教授，研究方向为性别政治、女性在政治生活中面临的壁垒，以及政治文化的相关性和根源。

31. **塔尔科特·帕森斯**（1902—1979），20世纪欧美最具影响力的社会学家之一，他在海德堡大学获得博士学位，并与韦伯的朋友哲学家卡尔·雅斯贝斯、韦伯的弟弟阿尔弗雷德·韦伯、古典社会学家卡尔·曼海姆一起从事研究，1930年出版译著《新教伦理与资本主义精神》，代表作为《社会系统》（1951）。

32. **威廉·佩蒂爵士**（1623—1687），英国政治经济学家，其著述主要涉及国家在经济中的作用，他还曾当过医生、音乐教授和英国议员。

33. **费利克斯·拉赫福尔**（1867—1925），研究德国和荷兰的历史学家，曾与韦伯就《新教伦理和资本主义精神》开展论辩。

34. 海因里希·里克特（1863—1936），新康德主义西南学派的领军人物，也是韦伯的朋友，代表作为《自然科学概念形成的限制》两卷本（1896、1902）。

35. 沃尔夫冈·施鲁赫特（1938年生），德国社会学家中研究韦伯的领军人物，德语版《马克斯·韦伯全集》的编辑，代表作为《现代理性主义的产生：韦伯关于西方发展史的分析》（1979）。

36. 格奥尔格·西梅尔（1858—1918），哲学家，也是最重要的古典社会学家之一，和韦伯共同创立了德国社会学会，代表作为《大都市与精神生活》（1903）和《货币哲学》（1907）。

37. 维尔纳·桑巴特（1863—1941），马克思主义经济学家、社会学家。他因与韦伯在现代资本主义研究上的不同见解而闻名于英语社会学界，其代表作为《为什么美国没有社会主义》（1906）。该书研究了美国的特例——美国精神与其他工业化国家不同，特别是其政治思想。

38. 理查德·斯威德伯格（1948年生），在美国工作的瑞典社会学家，代表作为《马克斯·韦伯和经济社会学思想》（2000）。

39. 亚历克西·斯·托克维尔（1805—1859），法国政治学家、历史学家，代表作为《论美国的民主》两卷本（1835，1840）。

40. 恩斯特·特勒尔奇（1865—1923），神学家，代表作为《基督教社会思想史》（1911）。韦伯认为该书是对其研究的确认和补充。

41. 布莱恩·特纳（1945年生），英国澳裔社会学家，代表作为《身体与社会》（1984）。他还参与编著马克斯·韦伯的《经济与社会》，主编的《经典社会学》期刊经常刊发有关韦伯的最新研究。

42. 玛丽安娜·韦伯（1870—1954），马克斯·韦伯的妻子，社会学和女权主义学者。在丈夫去世后，她整理和结集出版了韦伯未发表的著述，包括他的巨著《经济与社会》，并写下了传世的《韦伯传》（1926）。

43. 威廉·文德尔班（1848—1915），新康德主义西南学派的另一位领军人物，代表作为《哲学史教程》（1893）。

44. 卢德格尔·沃斯曼因，慕尼黑大学的德国经济学家，研究方向为长期繁荣和学生成就的决定因素。

WAYS IN TO THE TEXT

- A pioneer in the field of sociology* (the study of the history and functioning of society), Max Weber was born in 1864 in Prussia;* he wrote *The Protestant Ethic* after having a nervous breakdown.

- *The Protestant Ethic* argues that religious ideas help explain how societies form different economic and social structures.

- Critics consider *The Protestant Ethic* one of the classic works of twentieth-century sociology.

Who Was Max Weber?

The author of *The Protestant Ethic and the Spirit of Capitalism*, Max Weber was one of the founders of modern sociology; he remains one of the most important thinkers of the twentieth century. Born in 1864 in the city of Erfurt, near the center of modern Germany, Weber's academic training focused on the law. In his doctoral dissertation and "habilitation"* thesis (a degree following a PhD), he explored matters concerning both economic and legal history. By the time he was 30, Weber had been appointed a professor of economics at the University of Freiburg.* Two years later, he moved to the University of Heidelberg.*

In 1897, Weber suffered a nervous breakdown, which forced him to abandon teaching until 1902 and again from 1903 to 1919. About five years after his breakdown, Weber recovered enough to write *The Protestant Ethic*. The essay held great personal significance for Weber. He strongly identified with the ascetic*— self-denying—character of the lonely and self-reliant Puritans* he described; the Puritans were a sect* of the Protestant* branch of modern Christianity who believed that the Roman Catholic* influence should be removed from Christian worship. In his wife's words, this was the first work to "make Weber's star shine again" and "connected with the deepest roots of his personality."[1]

Weber, who began to work on the main themes of *The Protestant Ethic* in 1898, wrote the essay between 1903 and 1905. It first appeared in the journal *Archiv für Sozialwissenschaften und Sozialpolitik** (Archives for Social Science and Social Policy) in two separate issues in 1904 and 1905. In 1919, Weber revised *The Protestant Ethic*, adding extended footnotes to address his critics. The final version was published in book form in 1920. Thanks to *The Protestant Ethic*, Weber remains a key figure in twentieth-century thought.

What Does *The Protestant Ethic* Say?

Weber asked if certain Protestant beliefs were linked with capitalism* (the social and economic system dominant in the West today in which trade and industry are held in private hands and exercised for profit). This important question challenged the prevailing arguments of the time, suggesting that the features of capitalist societies came from preexisting economic conditions or material interests. Weber contended that ideas mattered too and were not subordinate to economic interests. He argued that we cannot trace the existence of a "spirit of capitalism"* simply to material or economic interests; because we can find this spirit only among certain groups, in certain regions and periods, we must examine other factors.

For Weber, the "spirit of capitalism" must, rather, be associated with the types of beliefs held by particular groups of people. He decided that the beliefs in question were most probably religious, since Roman Catholics and Protestants clearly diverged in their work ethics. Weber determined that Roman Catholics were less likely to be involved in business or the professions than Protestants. They were also generally less well-off than Protestants. He argued that this difference resulted from Roman Catholics' religiously based cultural orientation, which rendered them less suited to business than their Protestant neighbors.

Weber also noted that the capitalism of Western Europe and the United States was distinct from capitalism as practiced elsewhere in the world. Western capitalism retained specific characteristics: it organized free labor in a rational, calculated manner and pursued profit systematically. To understand the origins of capitalism, Weber argued, we should inquire about the origins of the "spirit" that guides it. Since this spirit seemed common among Protestants, Weber intended to find out if and how religious beliefs affected capitalism.

Weber suggested that some Protestant sects encouraged ascetic work—work conducted without concern for pleasure—for profit. These included the idea of work as a calling* as proposed by Martin Luther* (a vitally important figure in the founding of Protestant Christianity in the sixteenth century), and the Calvinist* idea of predestination.* "Calvinism" is a branch of Protestantism holding specific interpretations of certain Christian beliefs; "predestination" is the idea that God has already decided the course of events, notably who will make it to Heaven and who will not.

In both sects, individuals embraced work as way of demonstrating that they were "chosen" by God. Weber argued that this ethic had also become secular* (that is, nonreligious). This secularized version of the Protestant ethic had contributed to the rise of Western capitalism since the eighteenth century, when the doctrines of predestination and the virtue of ascetic work became popular.

Since the time of its publication, sociologists have both widely praised and criticized Weber's work. Authors proposing alternative theories about the origins of modern capitalism place themselves at the heart of a major debate when they confront the "Weber thesis." But while many claim the text is historically wrong and too imaginative, these criticisms have not affected the work's reputation. Rather, Weber's thought-provoking ideas and the original paths of research that they can inspire have made the work a classic.

Why Does *The Protestant Ethic* Matter?

The Protestant Ethic remains important for the originality of both its argument and its methodology. The work has become a foundational and highly influential piece in the discipline of sociology. Indeed, some may hold it as the most important piece. Scholars generally regarded it as a great exemplar of theoretically creative empirical* scholarship—that is, research capable of being verified or disproved through observation or experiment. It is hard to overstate the importance of Weber's thesis.

But the work does not remain relevant because of its historical accuracy; indeed, many disagree with Weber's analysis of history. It remains relevant because the development of modern capitalism has become a central issue in sociology. Other founders of the discipline, such as the nineteenth-century German political philosopher Karl Marx* and the pioneering French sociologist Émile Durkheim,* have also addressed this issue. Some see Weber's work as a critique of Marx's "historical materialist"* theory of industrial capitalism. Marx stressed the importance of material conditions in determining the economic and class structure of societies; Weber offered a counterpoint, making the case that ideas were significant also.

Beyond sociology, *The Protestant Ethic* has inspired important works in many other fields and subfields, such as the sociology of organizations.* This is the study of formal and informal institutions, influenced by Weber's analysis of bureaucracy;* its practitioners analyze the structure of these institutions and how these institutions determine the way individuals interact.

While some scholars still challenge the claims of *The Protestant Ethic*, sociologists today remain more concerned with using it to inspire new areas of research. The book has arguably become the most frequently cited source for ideas about the role that religious beliefs play in attitudes toward work—a fact that stems, naturally, from Weber's main thesis that the religious beliefs of certain Protestant sects could explain the development of modern capitalism. *The Protestant Ethic* has also become influential in the study of modernization and the rationalization* of society (that is, the move toward a social life governed by rational decisions and assumptions). Weber argues that the process of rationalization— particularly the rationalization of work—forms a distinctive part of the movement to modern capitalism.

---

1 Marianne Weber, *Max Weber: A Biography*, trans. Harry Zohn (New Brunswick, NJ: Transaction Publishers, 1988), 335.

SECTION 1
INFLUENCES

THE AUTHOR AND THE HISTORICAL CONTEXT

KEY POINTS

- A revolutionary text, *The Protestant Ethic* attempted to explain the development of modern capitalism.*
- Weber felt a great affinity with the asceticism*—the practice of self-denial—of the Puritans.*
- Weber sought to explain the development of modern capitalism at the start of the twentieth century.

Why Read *The Protestant Ethic*?

Max Weber's *The Protestant Ethic and the Spirit of Capitalism* remains one of the most important works of sociology* written in the twentieth century. Because Weber uses empirical* data to shape his argument (that is, data verifiable by observation), many believe the work has played a large role in establishing the academic discipline of sociology. Still, *The Protestant Ethic* remains relevant not just because of its methodological approach, but because of Weber's argument.

Weber asks why certain groups engage in different types of economic behavior. Two other founders of sociology, the political philosopher Karl Marx* and the French thinker Émile Durkheim,* had also engaged with this question. Weber argued that the ideas associated with certain religious groups determined economic behavior and the economic structure of societies. This directly critiqued Marx's "historical materialist"* theory, according to which material conditions shaped the economic organization of societies. Weber instead suggested that the role of ideas should not be neglected.

Weber made a crucial and enduring contribution to scholarship by arguing that the beliefs of certain Protestant* groups could help explain the development of the economic and social system of modern capitalism.* While critics have challenged some of the empirical claims of *The Protestant Ethic* (that is, its scientific findings), it remains one of the most widely cited works discussing the role of ideas in the development of modern capitalism. As the British sociologist Anthony Giddens* comments: "*The Protestant Ethic and the Spirit of Capitalism* undoubtedly ranks as one of the most renowned, and controversial, works of modern social science." [1]

> "Throughout his life Weber saw himself as a 'bourgeois scholar' with a sense of mission."
>
> Kieran Allan, *Max Weber: A Critical Introduction*

Author's Life

Max Weber was born in 1864 in Erfurt, Prussia* (a state incorporated into modern-day Germany and Poland) and died in 1920 in Munich, Germany. Weber had a tense relationship with his father, an important figure in German politics. His mother, very influenced by American Unitarianism* and English Progressive* Christianity (both strands of Protestant theology*), played a significant role in helping Weber develop his ideas about the Protestant ethic. Her activism in liberal religious circles inspired Weber to inquire about morality and made him aware of the role moral standards play in guiding an honorable life.

Although Weber's academic background centered primarily in the law, he wrote his doctoral thesis on economic and legal history. This led him to a career as a professor of economics—first at the University of Freiburg* in 1894 and then two years later at the University of Heidelberg.* After Weber's father died in 1897, he had a nervous breakdown that forced him to abandon teaching almost completely. He began to write *The Protestant Ethic* between 1903 and 1905. The highly influential journal *Archiv für Sozialwissenschaften und Sozialpolitik*[*2] published it in two separate issues in 1904 and 1905. In 1920, *The Protestant Ethic* was published in book form with extended footnotes addressing its critics.

The work had particular significance to Weber, who personally identified with the moral outlook of the Protestant groups he described. While other scholars might have arrived at the same arguments, Weber's personal connection to the concepts in *The Protestant Ethic* gave him important insights that other thinkers may have missed.

Author's Background

At the turn of the twentieth century, Germany (and many other parts of Europe) stood at a crossroads between its premodern* past and its modern present. Industrialization had not yet reached its countryside and villages, so in some ways the past remained on display. The cities, on the other hand, were rapidly industrializing. They represented modernity and the future. This divide inspired many studies of the period. Scholars asked how we could live and guide our lives under capitalism, which they saw as a system in which the market takes priority over tradition, ethical values, and personal relationships. In *The Protestant Ethic* Weber aimed in part to explain how modern capitalist society developed from more traditional forms of economic organization.

Another social issue of the period relevant to Weber's essay was discrimination (or the perception of discrimination). German Catholics, feeling they were underrepresented in civil-service jobs, lobbied for a quota system.Weber believed that Catholics held fewer business and professional jobs not because of discrimination but because of their religiously based cultural orientation. He saw Roman Catholic culture as less suited to business than Protestant. The nineteenth-century French historian Alexis de Tocqueville* had suggested in his work *Democracy in America* that religion affected economic behavior.[3] But social scientists had not yet addressed the issue in a systematic manner. This practical problem motivated Weber to write an essay that contributed not only to the understanding of the social basis of economic life, as it is often understood today, but also to the policy debates of the period.

1 Max Weber, *The Protestant Ethic and the Spirit of Capitalism*, trans. Talcott Parsons (London: Routledge, 2005), vii.

2 *Archiv für Sozialwissenschaften und Sozialpolitik* (Archives for Social Science and Social Policy) was edited by Weber, Werner Sombart and Edgar Jaffé, and became the leading German journal of the time.

3 Victor Nee and Richard Swedburg, *On Capitalism* (Stanford, CA: Stanford University Press, 2007), 54.

MODULE 2
ACADEMIC CONTEXT

KEY POINTS

• When Weber wrote *The Protestant Ethic*, one of the most important academic concerns involved exploring the development of modern capitalism.*

• At the time, arguments influenced by Marxist* scholarship dominated the discussion and the social analysis, emphasizing the role of material interests—class and economics—in the formation of society.

• Weber challenged these prevailing arguments, stressing the role of ideas and not just material interests.

The Protestant Ethic in its Context

German social scientists and historians of the period were very much interested in the origins of capitalism and the process of industrialization, and Max Weber's *The Protestant Ethic and the Spirit of Capitalism* was one of the most significant contributions to this line of inquiry.

When it came to political thought and economics, the intellectual environment in Germany differed sharply from that in Britain during the same period. Referencing the philosophical approaches of utilitarianism,* according to which an action is judged "right" according to its effect, and idealism,* according to which "reality" is a question of perception and thought, the British sociologist* Anthony Giddens* says: "The dominant position of utilitarianism and classical political economy in [Britain] were not reproduced in Germany, where these were held at arm's length by the influence of idealism and, in the closing decades of the nineteenth century, by the growing impact of Marxism." [1]

The analytical approach of Karl Marx,* according to which material interests rather than *ideas*—religion and culture for example—determined the development of capitalism, was increasingly influential. But idealism remained the dominant methodology in Germany at the time; according to idealist principles human behavior could not simply be explained in terms of causal laws and instead "has to be 'interpreted' or 'understood' in a way which has no counterpart in nature."[2] This approach put a strong emphasis on the role of history in understanding human behavior because the "cultural values that lend meaning to human life ... are created by specific processes of social development."[3]

> "[Weber] was a member of the so-called 'younger generation' associated with the Verein,* the first group to acquire a sophisticated knowledge of Marxist theory and to attempt to creatively employ elements drawn from Marxism—without ever accepting it as an overall system of thought, and recoiling from its revolutionary politics."
>
> Anthony Giddens, Introduction to *The Protestant Ethic*

Overview of the Field

Many of Weber's contemporaries regarded the Marxist economist and sociologist Werner Sombart* as one of the most important voices on the development of modern capitalism. Sombart coedited the journal that published Weber's *The Protestant Ethic*. He published his most significant work, *Der Moderne Kapitalismus* (*Modern Capitalism*), in 1902. In *The Protestant Ethic,* Weber directly engaged with Sombart's arguments in *Der Moderne Kapitalismus*.

Sombart used Karl Marx's materialist theory* of historical change to describe how capitalism evolved from its feudalist* roots (feudalism being a medieval social system in which, very broadly, land ownership dictated status and wealth). He divided the capitalist period into three different sections. Early capitalism ended just before the Industrial Revolution* took hold in the mid-eighteenth century. High capitalism began in the mid-eighteenth century. And late capitalism started at the dawn of World War I.* Sombart continued the debate in 1911 with *The Jews and Modern Capitalism* and *The Quintessence of Capitalism: A Study of the History and Psychology of the Modern Business Man* (1913).

Like many thinkers at the time, Sombart emphasized material interests over ideas as the main cause of modern capitalism in Germany and the rest of Europe. Beyond the academic debates, some common ideas suggested rudimentary versions of a Protestant ethic hypothesis—most notably the idea that religious beliefs affected work habits. Additionally, journalists and the educated public acknowledged a relationship between occupational status and religion. In a 1902 discussion of the relationship between the Protestant sect* of Calvinism* and the development of capitalism, Sombart commented that it was "too well-known a fact to require detailed explanation."[4] But social scientists had not studied this relationship in detail until Weber took up the challenge. Weber responded to Sombart—and to other critics—in extended footnotes to the 1920 book edition of *The Protestant Ethic*, as well as in other works.

Academic Influences

After moving to Heidelberg* in 1896, Weber met other important philosophers and social scientists. They became part of the so-called Weber circle, which included intellectuals such as Georg Jellinek,* Ernst Troeltsch* (both of whom influenced *The Protestant Ethic*), Werner Sombart, and the woman who would become Weber's wife—the sociologist and women's rights activist Marianne Weber.* Max Weber's influence also brought many other scholars to Heidelberg. One of the most important of these was the now almost forgotten German economist and historian Eberhard Gothein.* While the Weber circle did not constitute a cohesive school of thought, some of its members significantly influenced *The Protestant Ethic*. In addition to Sombart, Weber also engaged with Edgar Jaffé,* another of his coeditors on the *Archiv für Sozialwissenschaft und Sozialpolitik*. Ernst Troeltsch guided Weber's secondary readings about the sociological implications of the Calvinist world view. Perhaps most importantly, Eberhard Gothein's *Economic History of the Black Forest* (1892) called Weber's attention to the role Calvinism played in the spread of capitalism. Yet Weber recalls that Jellinek's *The Declaration of the Rights of Man and Citizens* (1895) inspired him "to take up the study of Puritanism* once again."[5] Jellinek encouraged Weber to pay attention to the effects of religion—generally not the first place scholars of capitalism would look.

Other scholars who had an important influence on Weber, particularly in 1903 when he began to work on the epistemological* foundations of sociology (that is, the role of thought and ideas in the formation of society), were the neo-Kantians*—followers of the thought of the influential eighteenth-century German philosopher Immanuel Kant—and related intellectuals. The most notable of these were Heinrich Rickert,* Wilhelm Windelband,* Wilhelm Dilthey,* and Georg Simmel.* These philosophers distinguished between the human or cultural sciences and the positivist* natural sciences; for positivists, only knowledge that can be verified by experience is valid. Weber and Simmel developed an interpretative sociology,* or sociology of understanding (*verstehen*)—that stood in contrast to French positivist sociology. Rather than seeking to describe facts, it sought to explain the causes and consequences of actions by understanding the subjective *meaning* of actions—the meaning of work for Protestants, for example.

1 Max Weber, *The Protestant Ethic and the Spirit of Capitalism*, trans. Talcott Parsons (London: Routledge, 2005), VIII.

2 Weber, *The Protestant Ethic and the Spirit of Capitalism*, IX.

3 Weber, *The Protestant Ethic and the Spirit of Capitalism*, IX.

4 Max Weber, *Economy and Society: An Outline of Interpretive Sociology*, ed. Guenther Roth and Claus Wittich (Berkeley, CA: University of California Press, 1978), LXXVI.

5 Max Weber, *The Protestant Ethic and the "Spirit" of Capitalism: And Other Writings*, trans. Peter Baehr and Gordon C. Wells (New York: Penguin, 2002), 155.

THE PROBLEM

KEY POINTS

* Academics in Weber's day focused on evaluating different factors associated with the development of modern capitalism.*

* The main arguments focused on material or rationalist* causes, as well as the roles of certain cultural groups.

* In *The Protestant Ethic*, Weber advanced an argument that the beliefs of certain Protestant* sects* had significant influence on the development of modern capitalism.

Core Question

In *The Protestant Ethic and the Spirit of Capitalism*, Max Weber sought to answer two core questions. The first was whether clear "elective affinities"* (a term denoting a kind of relationship or historical link) existed between certain Protestant beliefs and a "vocational* ethic" (roughly, a "work ethic"). Weber's precise focus here was whether or not there existed an affinity between the Protestant ethic and the "spirit of capitalism,"* by which he meant a way of organizing one's life around money, profit, and material success. This orientation toward work and economic gain did not exist in premodern economically "traditional" society: for a premodern culture work was a necessary evil, less valuable than leisure; people, then, were obliged to work only as required to meet traditional needs.

This core idea directly addressed the question of how modern capitalism had come to develop. Weber's argument rejected the materialist view of history* offered by Marxist*-influenced arguments, focusing on the role of economic interests. But Weber examined how particular ideas held by certain groups could help explain the development of modern capitalism.

Weber's second question also related to the development of modern capitalism. He wondered "to what degree the historical origins of central features of our modern life can be attributed to religious forces stemming from the Reformation* [the events that led to the formation of the modern Protestant branch of Christianity in the sixteenth century] and to what degree to other forces."[1] The answer would provide an understanding of the origins of capitalism that addressed the monumental cultural change that capitalism represented, especially in light of people's modern orientation toward economic action.

> "The proverb says jokingly, 'either eat well or sleep well'.
> In the present case the Protestant prefers to eat well, the
> Catholic to sleep undisturbed."
>
> Max Weber, *The Protestant Ethic*

The Participants

When Max Weber wrote *The Protestant Ethic*, the dominant literature in economic history denied that religion could influence an economic ethic. Traditional analysis held that modern capitalism stemmed from material interests and power, general evolution and progress, the business dealings of Jewish people, and abstract rationalism (the drive toward rational thought and behavior that defined modern societies), among other forces. Werner Sombart,* for example, stressed the role of Jews in the development of capitalism. He also held that capitalism represented one distinct stage in the rational development of societies. Others took Marx's work in another direction, seeing the development of capitalism in terms of class interests.

Economic historians tended not to focus systematically on interpreting the subjective "meanings" of economic action.Weber had not done this either in his own previous works. In fact, few professional historians discussed cultural history. The historian Eberhard Gothein*—who Weber had brought to Heidelberg* in 1904 to take over the chair in economic history he had vacated— remained one of the few exceptions to this rule. Gothein had floated the idea that the Protestant sect of Calvinism* helped spread capitalism; Weber extended this concept with a detailed analysis that specified the link between religious beliefs and capitalism from medieval Roman Catholicism* to the schism in the Christian religion known as the Reformation, and the theology* of Calvinism and the Protestant sects.

In doing this, *The Protestant Ethic* broke with the dominant literature in economic history; the work fitted well with the new discipline emerging in Germany: sociology.* The essay's focus on the interpretation of meanings became one of the foundations of the German tradition of "interpretative sociology,"* developed by Weber and the pioneering sociologist and philosopher Georg Simmel.*

The Contemporary Debate

In *The Protestant Ethic* Weber addressed many alternative theories of how modern capitalism had developed. He disagreed with Sombart's evolutionary thesis; indeed, that was one of Weber's main motivations for writing his essay. In contrast to Sombart, Weber suggested that changes do not develop in parallel in all spheres. Law emerged in the Middle Ages,* based on the principles of justice laid down in ancient Rome.* But modern capitalism developed in England, with a less rational form of law, the common law.* This undermines Sombart's argument.[2] Contrary to Marxist explanations, Weber claimed that the "spirit of capitalism" preceded the existence of a bourgeoisie (a middle class of business-owners) in the United States. In his view, capitalism was cultivated not so much by the commercial elite as by new entrepreneurs of middle-class origin. This analysis makes a simple class-based explanation of capitalism impossible.[3]

The Protestant Ethic received significant attention from thinkers in many disciplines. The most significant criticism came from the historians Felix Rachfahl* and H. Karl Fischer* who reviewed the essay in two journals, published in 1907 and 1909 respectively.Weber replied strongly to each of these reviews and to their authors' responses. He felt they lacked sufficient mastery of the topic to understand his work fully. Between 1911 and 1916, the economists Werner Sombart—also a sociologist—and Lujo Brentano* addressed *The Protestant Ethic* in larger works. Weber responded to them in extensive new footnotes to the

1920 book edition of *The Protestant Ethic*.While Weber clarified his arguments, he never changed any relevant ideas from those expressed in the original publication.

Sociologists both praised and criticized *The Protestant Ethic*. Beyond the discipline of sociology, scholars criticized it more often than praised it. These responses came from a wide range of disciplines, including history, economics, psychology, and even literary criticism. Many of the critics attacked the empirical* accuracy of Weber's arguments, such as his reading of the works of the American revolutionary Benjamin Franklin.*4 Nevertheless, authors proposing alternative theories about the origins of modern capitalism were forced to confront the "Weber thesis" if they wished to place themselves at the core of a major debate.

---

1 Weber, *The Protestant Ethic and the Spirit of Capitalism: With Other Writings on the Rise of the West*, trans. Stephen Kalberg, 4th ed. (New York: Oxford University Press, 2009), xxviii.

2 Fritz Ringer, *Max Weber: An Intellectual Biography* (Chicago: University of Chicago Press, 2010), 117.

3 Ringer, *Max Weber*, 115.

4 Ringer, *Max Weber*, 125.

MODULE 4
THE AUTHOR'S CONTRIBUTION

KEY POINTS

• Weber argued that religious ideas could help explain the development of the economic and social system of modern capitalism* through their effect on economic behavior.

• While some had written on this subject before Weber, he was the first thinker to link religious ideas to an explanation of modern capitalism.

• Weber wrote in response to the work of the Marxist* economist and sociologist* Walter Sombart,* and built upon the work of the philosopher of law Georg Jellinek* and the cultural historian Eberhard Gothein,* respectively.

Author's Aims

In writing *The Protestant Ethic and the Spirit of Capitalism*, Max Weber was motivated by skepticism about existing explanations of how modern capitalism developed. These explanations tended to treat cultural values "as passive forces generally subordinate to social structures, power, classes, evolution and progress, and economic and political interests."[1] Walter Sombart notably made this argument in his work *Der Moderne Kapitalismus* (1902). Weber also had great reservations about narratives that placed a few great individuals as the drivers of history.

Weber also attempted to explain the specific form Western capitalism had taken in terms of the "spirit of capitalism."* As Weber saw it, Western capitalism organized labor in a rational and calculated manner to better pursue profit. He suggested that the "spirit of capitalism" contributed to this by serving as a secular* "ethically oriented maxim" for the systematic "organization of life" around money, profit, work, competition, and material success as ends in themselves.[2] To understand the origins of capitalism, Weber felt we should examine the origins of its spirit. This spirit seemed prevalent among Protestants.* So Weber remained particularly interested in finding out whether and how religious beliefs could produce this spirit.

> *"The fate of our times is characterised by rationalisation and intellectualisation and, above all, by the 'disenchantment of the world'."*
>
> Max Weber, "Science as a Vocation"

Approach

In determining how modern capitalism developed, Weber examined how cultural values could determine the economic structure of societies—a kind of inquiry previously undertaken only at the margins of academia. Weber investigated the motivation for certain behaviors in large groups of people, wanting to uncover the "subjective meaning of social action." This became a central feature of his approach to historical interpretation throughout his work. By developing this interpretative sociology,* or sociology of understanding (*verstehen*), Weber rejected the approaches of positivism* and economic determinism* to understanding social phenomena. For positivists, only knowledge that could be verified by experience was valid; economic determinism holds that economic relationships are fundamental to explaining social phenomena (an idea associated with classic Marxist thought).

Weber became one of the first thinkers to explain the differences in economic behavior between Protestants and Roman Catholics. He did this by examining the meaning behind the actions of Protestant and Roman Catholic behavior and their religious origins. He argued that preexisting material conditions could not explain the economic choices prevalent in some regions within Germany; they could not explain, for example, why Protestants were generally wealthier than Roman Catholics.[3] Nor could they explain why Roman Catholics tended to study subjects in the humanities* rather than the business-oriented curriculum Protestants favored. It seemed clear to Weber that religious beliefs played an important role in determining people's economic behaviors; this, he believed, deserved serious investigation. His line of inquiry challenged the orthodoxy of the Marxist-influenced theories popular at the time, according to which material matters (economics, chiefly) were paramount in shaping society.

Contribution in Context

The idea of a causal link between Protestantism and capitalism diverged from mainstream scholarship of the time. It did not originate with Weber, however; he notes that the Spanish saw a link between Dutch Calvinism* and the promotion of trade. The British economist Sir William Petty* made a similar claim.[4]

The economic historian Eberhard Gothein's* depiction of the Calvinist diaspora*—the international spread of Calvinists—as the "seed bed of capitalist economy"[5] heavily influenced Weber's research.

Weber also wrote in reaction to the work of Werner Sombart. In *Der Moderne Kapitalismus* (1902), Sombart argued that material conditions within capitalism created certain ideas within Protestant sects.*[6] Weber, however, felt that Sombart got the cause and the consequence confused: for Weber, modern capitalism stemmed from "the spirit of capitalism" found within some elements of Protestantism. Another early writer who focused on the effect religion had on the structure of capitalism was the philosopher of law Georg Jellinek.* Weber's focus on Puritanism* resulted directly from the ideas Jellinek expressed in *The Declaration of the Rights of Man and Citizens* (1895). Jellinek, Sombart, Gothein, and others were part of what became known as the "Weber circle."While not a school of thought in its own right, many of its members contributed to Weber's thinking about the development of modern capitalism.

1   Max Weber, *The Protestant Ethic and the Spirit of Capitalism: With Other Writings on the Rise of the West*, trans. Stephen Kalberg, 4th ed. (New York: Oxford University Press, 2009), xxv–vi.

2   Weber, *The Protestant Ethic and the Spirit of Capitalism: With Other Writings on the Rise of the West*, 17.

3   Max Weber, *The Protestant Ethic and the Spirit of Capitalism*, trans. Talcott Parsons (London: Routledge, 2005), 4.

4 Weber, *The Protestant Ethic and the Spirit of Capitalism*, 10.

5 Weber, *The Protestant Ethic and the Spirit of Capitalism*, 10.

6 Werner Sombart, *Der Moderne Kapitalismus* "Modern Capitalism: A Historical and Systematic Exposition of Europe's Economic Life from Its Beginnings to the Present Day." No English translation is available.

SECTION 2
IDEAS

MODULE 5
MAIN IDEAS

KEY POINTS

- The key themes Weber addresses include the origins of the "spirit of capitalism"* within certain Protestant* sects* and how some religious ideas can explain the development of modern capitalism.*

- Weber argues that we can explain rationalized,* secular,* "modern" capitalism by looking at how the ideas of the Lutheran* and Calvinist* sects encouraged people to act.

- The first part of *The Protestant Ethic* explains the problem and the second analyzes it.

Key Themes

Weber begins his argument in *The Protestant Ethic and the Spirit of Capitalism* by observing that Protestants tended to be wealthier and more often involved in business than Roman Catholics.* He notes that "business leaders and owners of capital, as well as the higher grades of skilled labour, and even more the higher technically and commercially trained personnel of modern enterprises, are overwhelmingly Protestant."[1] This led Weber to his main hypothesis. He argued that something in the religious beliefs of Protestants—especially Calvinists and the followers of the German priest Martin Luther,* a key figure in the schism in the Christian religion that led to the founding of the religion's Protestant branch—led them to develop an economic ethic highly compatible with capitalist production.

The economic ethic of systematic work and the rational pursuit of profit has not existed everywhere or at all times. But it appeared in the West somewhat before the development of modern capitalism. To Weber this suggests that the "spirit of capitalism" has potentially played a role in sparking the development of modern capitalism.

Weber describes the conceptual foundations of "the spirit of capitalism" in Calvinism and other Protestant sects. He looks at John Calvin's* doctrine of predestination;* Calvin, a sixteenth-century French theologian,* taught that some people were destined to go to heaven and others—despite anything they might do in their lifetimes—would not. He argues that this created an unbearable despair among the devout: "a feeling of unprecedented inner loneliness of the single individual."[2] However, Calvinist theologians (scholars of religious thought and scripture) later revised the doctrine: believers who organized their life around methodical ascetic* work (work requiring self-denial) in a calling* and the pursuit of profit might enter heaven after all. This produced great psychological rewards for the faithful.

The sixteenth-century German cleric Martin Luther introduced the concept of a calling, claiming "every person had a 'calling' or 'vocation' given to him or her by God."[3] Weber believes this explains why Protestants remained more likely to be wealthy and to pursue a career in business.

Weber concluded his argument by explaining the historical link between the Protestant ethic and capitalism in more general terms. He argues that the ethos of ascetic work spread in the colonies that would become the United States in the eighteenth century. But in this new country it became secularized. Capitalism no longer needed the religious foundations of the spirit to reproduce itself: after society moved toward a rational basis, each individual would have no choice but to embrace capitalism:"Profit was now sought not to ensure one's state of grace, but because it was in one's self-interest to do so."[4]

> "The modern man is in general, even with the best will, unable to give religious ideas a significance for culture and national character which they deserve. But one can, of course, not aim to replace a one-sided materialistic with an equally one-sided spiritualistic causal interpretation of culture and of history."
>
> Max Weber, *The Protestant Ethic*

Exploring the Ideas

The Protestant Ethic contains three original and connected ideas. First, the importance of the "spirit" of modern capitalism and its origins in the Protestant ethic. Second, Luther's idea of work as a calling, and how Calvinist interpretations of the relationship between predestination and the calling motivated ascetic work in the pursuit of profit. Third, the secularized version of the Protestant ethic that had developed since the eighteenth century, especially in America. This sequence of ideas forms the core of the so-called "Weber thesis": the Protestant ethic created the orientation to work necessary for modern capitalism to develop, but today the explicit religious connection has been largely severed.

Without this work ethic contained in the "spirit of capitalism," Weber believes workers would only be motivated to work as much as necessary to satisfy traditional needs.[5] The origins of the Protestant ethic lie in Luther's idea of vocational* work as a calling: "labour in everyday life was seen as a God appointed task."[6] Luther's "this-worldly work" contrasted with the ascetic withdrawal from the world of Roman Catholic monks.

Those who adopted the ascetic ethic of Calvinism and the Protestant sects developed a closer "inner affinity"* with capitalism. They exalted success in the calling and in intensified labor. John Calvin's initial doctrine of predestination caused insufferable anguish among the faithful. But those who behaved in a manner that suggested they had been chosen, by embracing their calling, reaped significant psychological rewards from ascetic work. Other scholars before Weber had mentioned a relationship between Calvinism and capitalism. But they had not offered specific details of linkage.

In the eighteenth century, the ethos of ascetic work grew in the United States, but in a secularized fashion. The work, business, and ethics of American revolutionary politician Benjamin Franklin* offer a clear example of this. Franklin advised, for example, that "time is money"[7] and emphasized the importance of acting justly in financial affairs: "Remember this saying, *The good paymaster is lord of another man's purse*."[8] Ascetic work and wealth no longer earned a person's salvation. Instead they demonstrated good moral character and were values a community-oriented citizen should possess.Weber concluded that in revolutionary-era America, "victorious capitalism" no longer needed the idea of work as a calling to reproduce itself. Once a significant number of entrepreneurs organized their production in a modern capitalistic manner, competition would force the rest to follow or perish.

Scholars have used Weber's ideas to call attention to the importance of the cultural—and especially religious—foundations of orientations and motivations to work. His ideas have also illustrated the relationship between Protestantism and capitalism and, more broadly, rationalism.* The concept of rationalization* (the process in which actions calculated to achieve a given end are increasingly adopted) has been used to explain how social behaviors originally influenced by religious teachings can continue in secular societies.

Language and Expression

Weber targeted *The Protestant Ethic* at German social scientists and historians who fueled the academic debate about the origins of capitalism and industrialism. Because he did not aim to attract a lay audience, Weber writes in an academic style often using specialized language. For example, instead of using the words "free will," Weber instead uses the Latin phrase *liberum arbitrium*. The work is not, however, difficult to understand. His use of particular phrases perhaps relates to when the work was written, rather than the audience he aimed to reach.

Weber organized *The Protestant Ethic* into two straightforward parts. The briefer first part explains the research problem and its relevance. Part Two contains the analytic core and Weber's conclusions.

Weber's famous use of the term "iron cage"* was first found in a 1930 English translation of *The Protestant Ethic* made by the sociologist* Talcott Parsons.* Weber used the German term *"stahlhartes Gehäuse,"* or "iron cage," to describe the increasing rationalization of social and economic life in Western society. Some critics have argued, however, that rather than "iron cage," a more accurate translation may be "steel-hard casing." [9]

---

1   Max Weber, *The Protestant Ethic and the Spirit of Capitalism*, trans. Talcott Parsons (London: Routledge, 2005), 3.

2   Weber, *The Protestant Ethic and the Spirit of Capitalism*, 60.

3   Kieran Allen, *Max Weber: A Critical Introduction* (Pluto Press, 2004), 36.

4   Laura Desfor Edles and Scott Appelrouth, *Sociological Theory in the Classical Era: Text and Readings*, 3rd ed. (Thousand Oaks, CA: Sage, 2014), 166.

5   Weber, *The Protestant Ethic and the Spirit of Capitalism*, 24.

6   Allen, *Max Weber*, 36.

7   Weber, *The Protestant Ethic and the Spirit of Capitalism*, 14.

8   Weber, *The Protestant Ethic and the Spirit of Capitalism*, 15.

9   Peter Baehr, "The 'Iron Cage' and the 'Shell as Hard as Steel': Parsons, Weber, and the Stahlhartes Gehäuse Metaphor in the Protestant Ethic and the Spirit of Capitalism," *History and Theory* 40, no. 2 (2001): 153–169.

MODULE 6
SECONDARY IDEAS

KEY POINTS

* Weber's arguments have helped scholars criticize theories of history, such as those of Karl Marx,* founded on the role of material circumstances; they have contributed to cultural theories of economic development, and explained the role of the religious doctrine of predestination* in the development of capitalism.*

* Weber's work helped undermine the dominant Marxist* theories of his day.

* Weber's argument about the doctrine of predestination and the development of modern capitalism has had the greatest impact. This is thanks to its fundamental importance for the whole "Weber thesis."

Other Ideas

Max Weber supports each of his primary ideas in *The Protestant Ethic and the Spirit of Capitalism* with a series of secondary ideas. Many of these have influenced sociological* thought significantly. Weber claimed that capitalism itself could not have created the "spirit of capitalism."* Scholars have used this notion to argue against historical materialist* concepts, such as those of Karl Marx, with their emphasis on economic matters over ideas. Weber adds that even if capitalism could help to spread the "spirit," some force had to develop and sustain the idea that systematic pursuit of profit was desirable. The idea had to have a group, organization or class to serve as "social carriers."[1] That phrase is another influential concept Weber developed.

Weber argues that preexisting differences in the groups' material wealth cannot completely explain differences in economic attainment between Protestants* and Roman Catholics.* This notion influenced culturalist* explanations of inequality and poverty—explanations that seek to explain material circumstances by looking at the role of culture; some argue, for example, that understanding different cultural attitudes toward economic behavior can help us account for differences in development throughout the world.[2] The German economist Sascha O. Becker* suggested that Weber's analysis of Protestant and Roman Catholic attitudes can even help explain contemporary economic problems in the eurozone* (the parts of Europe in which the euro is the currency).[3] Generally Protestant northern European countries exhibit more financial prudence than Roman Catholic Mediterranean countries. According to this view, cultural attitudes determine these countries' varying economic situations.When these attitudes clash, political crises ensue.

> "We can clearly identify the traces of the influence of the doctrine of predestination in the elementary forms of conduct and attitude toward life in the era with which we are concerned, even where its authority as a dogma was on the decline."
>
> Max Weber, *The Protestant Ethic*

Exploring the Ideas

The most important secondary idea Weber raises involves the sociological effects surrounding the concept of salvation (the Christian doctrine according to which God saves the worthy from eternal damnation), especially its material consequences. This became a central element in Weber's subsequent works in the sociology of religion, which have remained influential. He traces how Roman Catholics, Lutherans,* Calvinists,* and the other sects* of the Protestant branch of Christianity dealt with the problem of salvation. Catholics believe that sins can be forgiven in confession, allowing even former sinners to attain salvation. But Protestant sects took a harder line on sin—especially the Calvinists, who preached predestination (according to which the fate of the individual's soul is entirely decided by God). So how could they ease the anxieties of the faithful worried about salvation? They turned to the notion of rational work as a calling*—a God-given task. This gave religious meaning to work previously considered mundane.

Calvin's "doctrine of predestination" produced widespread hopelessness among believers, since they could not know or control the eventual fate of their soul. So theologians* and ministers of later Christian sects, among them the Pietist,* Methodist,* Quaker,* and Baptist* sects, reinterpreted the doctrine. Saved people, they suggested, exhibited four major qualities: first, the capacity for methodical work; second, the ability to create wealth and profit; third, becoming holy (or conducting themselves virtuously); fourth, feeling that they are possessed by God.[4] These signs offered great comfort to those who organized their life through methodical ascetic* work.

The British sociologist Ken Morrison explains how this created a "tendency among Protestants to distance themselves from the world."[5] A Protestant walked a solitary, God-given path to salvation. No outside influences could change this.[6] Furthermore, the ascetic approach to work put a "'psychological premium' on the regulation of one's own life that influenced the development of capitalism as a form of economic conduct."[7] So Calvin's doctrine not only affected the behavior of those who followed. It also established the conditions in which modern capitalism would develop.

Overlooked

Max Weber's *The Protestant Ethic* remains one of the most widely discussed works in the social sciences. It is hard to think of an aspect of the text that has not received attention. Scholars have extensively scrutinized its central and secondary arguments. And many of its ideas have inspired research in completely different areas. Scholars seem to have explored virtually all of the work's possible applications.

Nevertheless, some ideas have received more attention than Weber might have expected, and are attaining new significance. The most notable example is the metaphor that rationalization* of Western capitalism has constructed an "iron cage" in which individuals live. The influential sociologist Talcott Parsons* coined the term in his 1930 translation of the book; the first to be published in English, it has since become classic. Recent translators have criticized his word choice, however; for them, Weber's phrase "*stahlhartes Gehäuse*" may be more accurately translated as "steel-hard casing"[8] or "shell as hard as steel."[9] Nevertheless, Parsons's concept has achieved a special significance and resonance of its own, largely independent of the context in which Weber used the metaphor. It appears in the title of hundreds of sociological works, and scholars often apply it to rather unrelated topics, such as organizational analysis.[10]

---

1 Max Weber, *The Protestant Ethic and the Spirit of Capitalism: With Other Writings on the Rise of the West*, trans. Stephen Kalberg, 4th ed. (New York: Oxford University Press, 2009), LIII.

2 Lawrence E. Harrison and Samuel P. Huntington, *Culture Matters: How Values Shape Human Progress* (New York: Basic Books, 2000).

3 Chris Arnot, "Protestant v Catholic: Which Countries Are More Successful?" *Guardian*, October 31, 2011, accessed September 5, 2015, http://www.theguardian.com/education/2011/oct/31/economics-religion-research.

4 Weber, *The Protestant Ethic and the Spirit of Capitalism: With Other Writings on the Rise of the West*, XXXV.

5 Ken Morrison, *Marx, Durkheim, Weber: Formations of Modern Social Thought* (Sage, 2006), 322.

6 Morrison, *Marx, Durkheim, Weber*, 322.

7 Morrison, *Marx, Durkheim, Weber*, 324.

8 Weber, *The Protestant Ethic and the Spirit of Capitalism: With Other Writings on the Rise of the West*, 158.

9 Max Weber, *The Protestant Ethic and the "Spirit" of Capitalism: And Other Writings*, trans. Peter Baehr and Gordon C. Wells (New York: Penguin, 2002), 121.

10 James R. Barker, "Tightening the Iron Cage: Concertive Control in Self-Managing Teams," *Administrative Science Quarterly* 38, no. 3 (1993): 408–437.

MODULE 7
ACHIEVEMENT

KEY POINTS

* *The Protestant Ethic* deeply influenced the establishment of the field of sociology.*

* Weber's empirical* approach gave weight to his original thesis demonstrating the effect of religious beliefs on economic behavior.

* Weber's argument may look less secure today because modern researchers have access to more—and different—sources of empirical data than Weber did at the turn of the twentieth century.

Assessing the Argument

With its highly original argument, Max Weber's *The Protestant Ethic and the Spirit of Capitalism* remains one of the most debated and celebrated works in the social sciences. Indeed, scholars consider it one of the foundational works in the discipline of sociology and a great example of empirical sociological research. Nevertheless, some might suggest that Weber did not achieve all he set out to do and many scholars have criticized the evidence that forms the basis of the "Weber thesis." For example, the German economists Sascha O. Becker* and Ludger Woessmann* argue that Protestant* economic success did not stem from the Protestant work ethic; for them, it can be explained by the much higher literacy rate among Protestants.[1] But, in Weber's defense, modern academics such as Becker and Woessmann have access to much more data than Weber did in his day.

But we cannot determine *The Protestant Ethic*'s contribution to scholarship solely by the accuracy of its empirical work. It remains important because of its contribution to the debate about the development of modern capitalism* in Germany, Western Europe more broadly, and the United States. Weber criticized Karl Marx's* influential argument that material (principally economic) factors were the primary engine for historical progress. Weber demonstrated that history had no rules, taking on an idea with many important adherents.

> "The Protestant Ethic and the Spirit of Capitalism *written in 1904–5, is probably the most important sociological work of the twentieth century.*"
>
> Daniel Bell, review of *The Protestant Ethic*

Achievement in Context

The influential journal *Archiv für Sozialwissenschaften und Sozialpolitik** (Archives for Social Science and Social Policy) published *The Protestant Ethic* in a series of journal articles in 1904 and 1905. Weber served as a coeditor of this journal, along with his sometime critic the Marxist economist and sociologist Wermer Sombart.* As it was one of the most famous and prestigious journals in Germany, Weber's work reached its intended audience with no difficulty. While *The Protestant Ethic* was only available in German until Talcott Parsons* translated it in 1930, meaning that English-speakers had to wait 25 years to access the work, the delay seems to have had little effect on its status.

Any empirical argument will be open to dispute when new evidence surfaces. For example, the Italian German economist Davide Cantoni* has argued that Protestantism and economic growth have no relationship: "Using population figures of 272 cities in the years 1300−1900, I find no effects of Protestantism on economic growth. The finding is precisely estimated, robust to the inclusion of various controls, and does not depend on data selection or small sample size."[2] But others claim evidence exists to support Weber's thesis. The economists Ulrich Blum* and Leonard Dudley* claim that between 1500 and 1750, wages fell in Roman Catholic* cities and increased in Protestant ones.[3] Nevertheless, the scholarly value of *The Protestant Ethic* does not rest solely on the accuracy of its empirical arguments.

Limitations

One of Weber's motivations in writing *The Protestant Ethic* was to understand and explain the roots of Western rationalization* (the process by which social behavior comes to be governed by rational decisions and behavior). Weber explained that the process of "rationalization in the West was advanced by a process he called calculation."[4] This meant that as economic values began to play a larger role in everyday life, assigning monetary values to things offered people greater control of the material world.[5] Weber used the process of rationalization to explain the specific form of capitalism that emerged in Western Europe and the United States.

In this sense we might argue that *The Protestant Ethic* only helps us analyze the economic conditions of Western Europe and the United States.

While Weber certainly argues that the Protestant ethic acted as a catalyst for the development of modern capitalism, he does not suggest that it is the only catalyst. As such, *The Protestant Ethic* has relevance beyond Europe and the United States because it raises the question of the potential link between religion and economic behavior. Weber addressed the issue in his major research project "Economic Ethics of the World Religions"[6]—with additional discussion in *Economy and Society* (1921)[7] and *General Economic History* (1923). Most notably, he analyzed why modern capitalism did not emerge in India or China. He looked at the role of religion and economic ethics, as well as material conditions, the law and the judicial system, among other factors.

Nevertheless, some scholars such as James Blaut,* an American professor of anthropology* and geography, have criticized Weber's ideas as Eurocentric* (that is, assuming the primacy of European experience and perspectives). In his view, Weber subscribes to a view of European exceptionalism—the belief that Europe is somehow a "special case"—that overestimates the uniqueness of Western rationalism* or of the "spirit of capitalism."[8] Scholars have also criticized Weber for attributing to other cultures a propensity for economic backwardness. As many of his time did, he overlooked or undervalued non-Western elements of the culture. He did not account for the fact that European colonialism had oppressed some native cultures.

1 Sascha O. Becker and Ludger Woessmann, "Was Weber Wrong? A Human Capital Theory of Protestant Economic History," Program on Education Policy and Governance, Harvard University (2007).

2 Davide Cantoni, "The Economic Effects of the Protestant Reformation: Testing the Weber Hypothesis in the German Lands," *Journal of the European Economic Association* 13, no. 4 (2014): 561.

3 Ulrich Blum and Leonard Dudley, "Religion and Economic Growth: Was Weber Right?" *Journal of Evolutionary Economics* 11, no. 2 (2001): 207–30.

4 Ken Morrison, *Marx, Durkheim, Weber: Formations of Modern Social Thought* (London: Sage, 2006), 284.

5 Morrison, *Marx, Durkheim, Weber*, 284–5.

6 This was a major project that Weber worked on mainly between 1911 and 1914, but which he completed in 1920 with the German publication of his *Collected Essays in the Sociology of Religion*. Among the main works here are *The Protestant Ethic*, *The Religion of China* (1915), *The Religion of India* (1916), *Ancient Judaism* (1917), and the "Introduction to the Economic Ethics of the World Religions" (1920).

7 Max Weber, *Economy and Society: An Outline of Interpretive Sociology*, ed. Guenther Roth and Claus Wittich (Berkeley: University of California Press, 1978).

8 J. M. Blaut, *Eight Eurocentric Historians* (New York: Guilford Press, 2000), 29.

PLACE IN THE AUTHOR'S WORK

KEY POINTS

* Weber's life's work involved investigating the development of Western capitalism.*

* *The Protestant Ethic* was Weber's first attempt to explain this development.

* *The Protestant Ethic* established Weber as one of the most influential thinkers of the twentieth century.

Positioning

The Protestant Ethic and the Spirit of Capitalism represents the first major piece in Max Weber's mature phase of production. In this period, and after his recovery from a nervous breakdown, he turned toward interpretative sociology:* an approach to the field that, rather than focusing on describing facts, seeks to explain the causes and consequences of actions by understanding their subjective *meaning*. After publication of *The Protestant Ethic* in 1905,Weber continued to investigate the effects of religion on economic behavior and social structure in his article "The Protestant Sects and the Spirit of Capitalism" (1906). Inspired by his 1904 trip to the United States, the article analyzed the relation between Protestantism* and capitalism in that country at the turn of the twentieth century.

Weber noted that in the United States, Protestantism encouraged the development of capitalism. He attributed this to psychological inducements connected with the concept of predestination* created by the beliefs held by certain Protestant sects* (that is to say, he argues that people acted as if they were chosen because this made life more bearable). But these inducements also existed in Europe. In the United States, Weber argued, Protestant churches also created a certain group discipline that reinforced moral economic behavior favoring capitalist development. These disciplines included paying debts on time and charging fair prices. Weber saw this behavior in the United States as paving the way for the capitalist spirit to transform into a secular* work ethic; eventually, this work ethic encompassed the whole of society and was not limited to certain Protestant sects.

With his essay on the Protestant sects in the United States, Weber began to extend his original argument. First, he moved beyond an analysis of Christian religions, broadening the scope of his comparative work. In his project "Economic Ethics of the World Religions," developed between 1911 and 1914, looking at non-Western religions including Hinduism,* Buddhism,* Confucianism,* Taoism,* and Judaism* (a religion with its roots in the Middle East), Weber examined how each shaped the way their believers related to economic issues. To him, this explained why capitalism did not develop outside the West, notably in India and China.

> "The Protestant Ethic *constituted the first full length study published by Weber, and as a result it became the centerpiece of the author's major investigative work.*"
>
> Ken Morrison, *Marx, Durkheim, Weber: Formations of Modern Social Thought*

Integration

After publication of *The Protestant Ethic*, Weber began to focus on other factors that could cause the development of capitalism and the process of Western rationalization.* He did not suggest that religion can explain everything relating to the development of modern capitalism. Instead, he emphasized that material conditions also had an important role to play. Weber developed his research on the rise of Western capitalism in both *Economy and Society* (1921) and *General Economic History* (1923).

He argued that other factors also played a role in the development of Western capitalism. These included rational accounting* methods and price-setting to generate profit, and a system of law with calculable results. All of these developed in the West at roughly the same time as capitalism. Comparing the West to other regions across the globe further highlighted the importance of these nonreligious factors. For instance, Weber noted that the lack of "formally guaranteed law and a rational administration and judiciary" in China created obstacles to capitalist development.[1]

Analyzing the role of religion and other factors in the unique development of rational capitalist economic organization in the West might seem an ambitious project. But Weber did not stop there. He became involved in even more ambitious research, focusing on the rise of rationality in Western culture. In this he included the development of the capitalist economy, formal, rational law, and the bureaucratic* state.

As for how *The Protestant Ethic* fits with Weber's broader

concerns, the British sociologist Ken Morrison notes, "Some of the shortcomings in Weber's overall body of works meant that his writings as a whole have generally not been viewed as a unified body of work organized as a complete thematic whole."[2] Indeed, commentators such as the German sociologist Friedrich Tenbruck have argued that it is difficult to find any thematic unity throughout Weber's work.[3]

Significance

The Protestant Ethic stands as a major piece in Weber's impressive and influential body of work on the development of Western capitalism and its unique form of rationalism.* Many scholars feel that Weber's arguments in *The Protestant Ethic* remain open to criticism. But few deny the importance of his contribution to the debate around the development of modern capitalism—and the ingenuity of his approach.

Weber's first attempt to systematically explain the roots of modern capitalist society, *The Protestant Ethic*, remains his best-known work. Ken Morrison suggests "it was viewed as a classic as soon as it was published."[4] Largely because of the originality of his argument, the work also helped Weber establish his reputation as one of the founders of the discipline of sociology. As the sociologist Kieran Allen indicates, *The Protestant Ethic* "is regarded by many sociologists as one of the key texts in their discipline."[5] Weber's empirical* approach involved careful and detailed historical research. This novel manner of working shaped the way sociological research is conducted today. The publication, and later the translation, of *The Protestant Ethic* established Weber as one of the most important thinkers of the twentieth century. This reputation has not diminished.

---

1 Max Weber, *The Religion of China: Confucianism and Taoism*, trans. Hans H. Gerth (New York: Free Press, 1951), 85.

2 Ken Morrison, *Marx, Durkheim, Weber: Formations of Modern Social Thought* (London: Sage, 2006), 275.

3 Friedrich H. Tenbruck, "The Problem of Thematic Unity in the Works of Max Weber," *British Journal of Sociology* 31, no. 3 (1980): 316–51.

4 Morrison, *Marx, Durkheim, Weber*, 313.

5 Kieran Allen, *Max Weber: A Critical Introduction* (Pluto Press, 2004), 32.

SECTION 3
IMPACT

THE FIRST RESPONSES

KEY POINTS

- Critics have accused Weber of ignoring other causal factors in the development of capitalism* and overestimating the role Protestantism* played in establishing the "spirit of capitalism."*

- Weber responded that he was not trying to provide a comprehensive explanation of the development of capitalism. He also defended the link between Protestant sects* and the "spirit of capitalism."

- Thanks to the originality of Weber's thesis, the work had a very positive reception.

Criticism

The historians H. Karl Fischer* and Felix Rachfahl* wrote detailed critiques of Max Weber's *The Protestant Ethic and the Spirit of Capitalism*, first published in journals. The German economists Lujo Brentano* and Werner Sombart* also criticized the work in their own books; Sombart, both an economist and a sociologist,* was one of Weber's coeditors at the journal that published Weber's work.

Critics called Weber's work one-sided. Some felt he did not fully explain the origins of capitalism. Others held that Weber focused too much on the role of ideas, ignoring other potential factors. Sombart argued that Jewish people had formed the vanguard of capitalism: "Now, if Puritanism* has had an economic influence, how much more so has Judaism,* seeing that among no other civilized people has religion so impregnated all national life."[1] Brentano offered a more specific criticism. He suggested that something like the "spirit of capitalism" existed among Roman Catholic* Italian merchants, centuries before the Reformation.* Brentano argued that "the Italian merchant cities of Venice, Genoa, and Pisa were extremely capitalistic in their commercial operations and trading policies ... before Protestantism appeared."[2] Weber, however, does not take notice of this trend.

Fischer questioned the relationship between religion and the "spirit of capitalism," arguing that "neither the capitalist spirit nor the ideas on duty Weber associated with it could necessarily be said to have been affected by religious beliefs or writings."[3] Fischer suggested that Weber did not consider strongly enough the argument that political and social forces might create the "spirit of capitalism."[4] Fischer felt that during the Reformation, ideas had changed to suit the changing economic circumstances.[5] In his view, this could have caused the link between Protestantism and capitalism.

Rachfahl also took issue with Weber's thesis, claiming "Weber had not provided sufficient evidence to substantiate his own thesis and thus failed to formulate the relationship between Protestantism and capitalism correctly."[6] Rachfahl suggests that capitalism in the Netherlands developed before Calvinism,* and many of the capitalists at the time were Roman Catholics. This was also the case in England before the Protestant sect of Puritanism took root. He claimed Weber provided little evidence that Puritan commercial activity had religious motivations.[7]

> *"In a way, the controversy over Weber's* Protestant Ethic
> *began even before the essay was first published"*
>
> Fritz Ringer, *Max Weber: An Intellectual Biography*

Responses

Weber replied to critics in a series of "anti-critical responses" that appeared in the *Archiv für Sozialwissenschaften und Sozialpolitik,** the journal that had first published *The Protestant Ethic*.[8] He also responded in the full edition of *The Protestant Ethic* published in 1920.

Weber found Fischer's and Rachfahl's critiques irrelevant. It had never been his objective to totally explain the origins of capitalism; he had only wanted to inquire about the *link* between Protestantism and modern capitalism. Furthermore, he had never doubted that capitalism existed long before Calvinism. He stressed this more modest objective throughout the text and in the concluding pages.Weber also accepted his critics were correct that many of the factors they cited had helped to develop capitalism.[9]

In notes to the 1920 book edition of the essay, Weber addressed Brentano's argument that he had overlooked Roman Catholic entrepreneurs in the medieval and Renaissance periods. He maintained that Protestants, not their Roman Catholic predecessors, had introduced the methodical aspect of the capitalist economic ethic.This methodical element had provided the "intensity" of work required to break with "economic traditionalism."*[10]

To Sombart's claim that Jews had developed a norm of

132

capitalist acquisition, Weber argued that the outsider or "pariah" status of Jews meant that they wielded less influence in society than the Puritans.[11] In Weber's view, Jews accepted this outsider status so they could maintain a "ritual purity": only "shady economic dealing with the outsider was acceptable."[12] The outsider status of Jews excluded them from "economic activity consistent with the continuous, systematic, and rationalized* industrial enterprise."[13]

Citing the academic discipline of philology* (the study of languages, involving literary criticism, history, and linguistics), Weber accused Fischer of failing to provide any compelling evidence for *his* arguments: "Philological findings may obviously correct my conclusions at any time. However, as the evidence stands, this certainly cannot be done by merely asserting the opposite."[14] Fischer replied that Weber should seek to discount all the other possible explanations so he could prove religion was the most important factor in determining economic behavior. Weber responded that this would be impossible and would involve him having to prove a negative.[15]

Weber took much the same approach in responding to Rachfahl's criticism.[16] He reasserted his argument that a person's religious vocation affects his or her conduct in life.[17] He also directed his critics to reread his original argument about the many causes of capitalism.[18]

Conflict and Consensus

The majority of the additions Weber made to the 1920 edition of *The Protestant Ethic* addressed the criticisms made by Sombart and Brentano. Although Weber treated their criticisms with more respect than he showed for Rachfahl's and Fischer's, he still dismissed them. In his additions to the 1920 text, Weber did not meaningfully change any essential elements of the 1905 essay; he only clarified his broader argument. This testifies to how strongly Weber felt about the arguments he made in *The Protestant Ethic.*

The Protestant Ethic stands as one of the most important and influential works of the twentieth century. So we should not be surprised that it has sparked an extraordinary amount of scholarship. Some academics still debate the validity of Weber's main thesis about the role Protestantism played in the development of modern capitalism. For example, the Italian German economist Davide Cantoni* has argued against Weber's thesis.[19] The Canadian economist Leonard Dudley* and the German economist Ulrich Blum,* on the other hand, have cited evidence supporting it.[20]

In general, scholars accept *The Protestant Ethic* as a classic and a foundational work. By now, more than a century after its original publication, only a few Weber specialists still debate the issues raised in *The Protestant Ethic*.

---

1 Werner Sombart, *The Jews and Modern Capitalism* (Kitchener, ON: Batoche Books, 2001), 134.

2 Paul D. Schafer, *Revolution or Renaissance: Making the Transition from an Economic Age to a Cultural Age* (Ottawa: University of Ottawa Press, 2008), 30.

3 Stephen P. Turner, *The Cambridge Companion to Weber* (Cambridge: Cambridge University Press, 2000), 163–4.

4 Turner, *The Cambridge Companion to Weber*, 164.

5 Turner, *The Cambridge Companion to Weber*, 164.

6 Turner, *The Cambridge Companion to Weber*, 164.

7 Turner, *The Cambridge Companion to Weber*, 164.

8 *Archiv für Sozialwissenschaften und Sozialpolitik* (Archives for Social Science and Social Policy) was edited by Weber, Werner Sombart, and Edgar Jaffé, and became the leading German journal of the time.

9 Turner, *The Cambridge Companion to Weber*, 162.

10 Hartmut Lehmann and Guenther Roth, *Weber's Protestant Ethic: Origins, Evidence, Contexts* (Cambridge: Cambridge University Press, 1995), 228.

11 Lehmann and Roth, *Weber's Protestant Ethic*, 230.

12 Lehmann and Roth, *Weber's Protestant Ethic*, 230–1.

13 Lehmann and Roth, *Weber's Protestant Ethic*, 231.

14 Sam Whimster, *Understanding Weber* (New York: Routledge, 2007), 119.

15 Whimster, *Understanding Weber*, 119.

16 Whimster, *Understanding Weber*, 120.

17 Whimster, *Understanding Weber*, 120.

18 Max Weber, *The Protestant Ethic and the Spirit of Capitalism*, trans. Talcott Parsons (London: Routledge, 2005), 49.

19 Davide Cantoni, "The Economic Effects of the Protestant Reformation: Testing the Weber Hypothesis in the German Lands," *Journal of the European Economic Association* 13, no. 4 (2014): 561–98.

20 Ulrich Blum and Leonard Dudley, "Religion and Economic Growth: Was Weber Right?" *Journal of Evolutionary Economics* 11, no. 2 (2001): 207–30.

THE EVOLVING DEBATE

KEY POINTS

- *The Protestant Ethic* had a deep impact on how people thought about the development of capitalism* and modern society.

- The schools of thought that emerged from the work included the functionalist* theories of Talcott Parsons* as well as conflict theories* inspired by Marxist* thought. "Functionalism" is a theoretical approach that considers society as a whole body composed of parts that contribute different functions to sustain it.

- *The Protestant Ethic* remains a foundational text in sociology* and continues to influence current scholarship.

Uses and Problems

Readings of Max Weber's *The Protestant Ethic and the Spirit of Capitalism* have changed significantly since its publication. The original debate concentrated on whether or not its thesis, now called the "Weber thesis," was factually correct. While this debate continued, sociologists began to focus more on the theoretical implications of Weber's findings, asking how different subfields could apply them.

The sociologist Talcott Parsons translated the work into English in 1930. That translation brought the work to wider attention in the global academic community. It was then—in the 1930s and 1940s—that *The Protestant Ethic* acquired its status as a foundational work in the field of sociology. Parsons translated and interpreted the text in a way that brought it closer to the French sociologist Émile Durkheim's* functionalism[1] (an approach that seeks to identify the useful "purpose" of the different forms of social behavior that constitute a society). But this interpretation also put Weber in opposition to Karl Marx,* underplaying the role of material interests and conflict in the development of capitalism.[2]

In the 1970s and 1980s, three of the most important contemporary sociological theorists—Pierre Bourdieu* in France, Anthony Giddens* in Great Britain, and Jürgen Habermas* in Germany—synthesized Marx, Weber, and Durkheim in their own theories of "practice," "structuration,"* and "communicative action,"* respectively.[3] In addition to drawing on Weber's ideas of domination and conflict, they also borrowed new ideas from *The Protestant Ethic*. They analyzed the "styles of life" developed in modern capitalism, recalling some of Weber's now-classic concepts such as the "disenchantment of the world"* (the idea that magical beliefs could not coexist with the increasingly rational nature of Western thought).

Today, most of the debates about *The Protestant Ethic* center not so much on its relevance for grand sociological theories, but on its applications in different subfields of sociology. Only scholars who specialize in interpreting Weber, including *The Protestant Ethic*, tend to go further than this. These include the British historian Peter Ghosh* and the Swedish sociologist Richard Swedberg.*

> "Capitalism is identical with the pursuit of profit, and forever renewed profit, by means of continuous, rational, capitalistic enterprise."
>
> Max Weber, *The Protestant Ethic*

Schools of Thought

Max Weber conceived *The Protestant Ethic* as a response to the Marxist* economist Werner Sombart's* 1902 work *Der Moderne Kapitalismus.* Scholars have traditionally seen the text, at least in part, as a critique of Marxist materialist conceptions of history.* But from the late 1950s, and especially in the 1960s and 1970s, the text began to influence Marxist-inspired sociologists, whose "conflict theories" bridged Marx and Weber and served as a counterpoint to Talcott Parsons's more functionalist interpretation.

Rather than stressing consensus over values, some scholars emphasized Weber's account of conflict, interests, domination, bureaucracy,* and rationality. These included the American sociologists C. Wright Mills* and Alvin Gouldner* and the German British sociologist Ralf Dahrendorf,* among others. Mills's *White Collar: The American Middle Classes*,[4] for example, expands on Weber's arguments about the process of bureaucratization (the increasing social importance of practices of administration in things such as government and business). In *Patterns of Industrial Behavior*,[5] Alvin Gouldner (a Marxist sociologist) discusses the extent to which bureaucracy could be used to dominate individuals. Weber has also inspired a number of scholars who may be called "pure Weberians." They do not synthesize his theory with those of other major authors; instead, they focus on interpreting Weber's work from the point of view of its original context and purposes, applying his ideas to help us understand other times and places.

German and British scholars remain notable in this tradition, with Reinhard Bendix* and Bryan S. Turner* among the most influential.

Various schools within subfields of sociology have also adopted *The Protestant Ethic*. For instance, in economic sociology* (inquiry into the ways in which economic behavior is embedded in society), the Swedish sociologist Richard Swedberg* argues, among other things, for assuming less rational* action and taking more seriously value-rational* and traditional, economic action ("value-rational" signifying an action performed for its inherent value, rather than to achieve a specific goal). This has been highly influential.[6]

In Current Scholarship

Scholars inspired by Weber continue to produce novel contributions, most notably in the areas of sociological theory, political science, and economic sociology. For example, the highly influential Indian anthropologist* Arjun Appadurai,* influenced by Weber's "spirit of capitalism,"* has written on the "spirit" of calculation.

Many of Weber's adherents, such as the German sociologist Wolfgang Schluchter,* have found that Weber's main contribution hinges on his understanding of Western rationalization—the process by which rational thought becomes increasingly predominant in social life. This process occurs in religion, work, accounting, politics, and law, although not always in a mutually related way. Jürgen Habermas finds that Weber's diagnosis of modern societies serves as the foundational sociological support for understanding rationally justifiable decisions. And he means this not only in terms of a philosophical ideal but also as an actual possibility. In other words, the sociological basis of Habermas's influential political theory of deliberative democracy* (a form of democracy in which decision-making is founded on discussion and reflections) owes much to Weber.[7]

Another scholar concerned with modernization and inspired by Weber is the American political scientist Ronald Inglehart.* Weber demonstrated that as countries become more capitalistic, their values shift. They move from traditional to modern materialist* values—those emphasizing economic and physical security— when their economies become more capitalistic. Inglehart takes this further. He argues that as wealthier countries continue to develop they embrace values concerned with self-expression and quality of life.[8] Taking a different approach, French sociologists Luc Boltanski* and his coauthor Ève Chiapello* note that capitalism still needs a spirit.They argue that in the modern world, most people do not seek this spirit in religion. Instead, they may find it in a class of managers and executives inspired by management ideology.[9]

In the discipline of economic sociology, Richard Swedberg has pioneered a Weber-inspired research program. He aims to provide an alternative to the focus on rational decisions and networks. By calling attention to the role of values and tradition in economic action, Swedberg has helped to redefine the subfield. Many other scholars have just made assumptions about these issues. Swedberg has also argued that Weber inspired Pierre

Bourdieu's important contributions to the subfield. He believes Bordieu's work on the "disenchantment of the world" and its relevance to understanding Algerian peasants owes something to Weber's *The Protestant Ethic*.[10]

---

1 Michele Dillon, *Introduction to Sociological Theory: Theorists, Concepts, and Their Applicability to the Twenty-First Century* (Chichester: John Wiley & Sons, 2009), 156.

2 Ken Morrison, *Marx, Durkheim, Weber: Formations of Modern Social Thought* (London: Sage, 2006), 295.

3 Paul Ransome, *Social Theory for Beginners* (Bristol: Policy, 2010), 291.

4 C. Wright Mills, *White Collar: The American Middle Classes* (Oxford: Oxford University Press, 2002).

5 Alvin W. Gouldner, *Patterns of Industrial Bureaucracy* (Free Press, 1964).

6 Richard Swedberg, *Max Weber and the Idea of Economic Sociology* (Princeton, NJ: Princeton University Press, 2000).

7 John P. McCormick, *Weber, Habermas and Transformations of the European State: Constitutional, Social, and Supranational Democracy* (Cambridge: Cambridge University Press, 2007), 30.

8 Ronald Inglehart, *Modernization and Postmodernization: Cultural, Economic, and Political Change in 43 Societies* (Princeton, NJ: Princeton University Press, 1997).

9 Luc Boltanski and Eve Chiapello, "The New Spirit of Capitalism," *International Journal of Politics, Culture, and Society* 18, no. 3–4 (2005): 161–88.

10 Richard Swedberg, "The Economic Sociologies of Pierre Bourdieu," *Cultural Sociology* 5, no. 1 (2011): 69.

MODULE 11
IMPACT AND INFLUENCE TODAY

KEY POINTS

* Scholars still consider *The Protestant Ethic* a classic text and a foundational piece of work in the discipline of sociology.*

* More than a century after its publication, *The Protestant Ethic* still fuels debate about the origins of modern capitalist* society.

* While some specialists continue to debate Weber's argument, most academic attention now focuses on applying Weber's ideas to new disciplines.

Position

Max Weber's *The Protestant Ethic and the Spirit of Capitalism* made a historic argument, as the British sociologist Peter Hamilton points out.[1] Weber wrote that "the religious root of modern economic humanity is dead; today the concept of the calling* is a *caput mortuum* in the world."[2] The Latin phrase literally translated as "dead head" serves to describe a "useless remnant." Since this constitutes Weber's main thesis, one might argue that *The Protestant Ethic* retains only limited relevance today. After all, Weber examined the development of capitalism. He did not concern himself with the state of the institution in our time, a hundred years later.

Yet *The Protestant Ethic* does remain relevant today, not because of its main argument but because it sparked a more general approach to thinking about social change. The American political scientist Francis Fukuyama* argues that while economists do not take Weber's cultural theory of economic growth particularly seriously, they still address his ideas concerning the role religion and culture play in the performance of institutions.[3] This useful insight can help explain contemporary issues such as differing attitudes toward corruption in Protestant* and Roman Catholic* countries.[4] Fukuyama also suggests that *The Protestant Ethic* has raised "profound questions about the role of religion in modern life."[5]

Furthermore, Weber's account of the rationalization* of Western society appears to have been accurate. We have seen, as he did, that "rational science based capitalism has spread across the globe, bringing material advancement to large parts of the world and welding it together in the iron cage* we now call globalization."[6] It would be an overstretch to say that the work stimulated new debates. But we can certainly use the ideas in *The Protestant Ethic* in contemporary debates about the relationship between religion and economic behavior. Fukuyama suggests that the "revival of Hinduism* among middle-class Indians ... or the continuing vibrancy of religion in America, suggests that secularization* and rationalism* are hardly the inevitable handmaidens of modernization."[7] This process does not exactly accord with Weber's argument in *The Protestant Ethic*, but it does illustrate the continued relevance of Weber's investigation.

Given the amount of attention *The Protestant Ethic* has received, it becomes nearly impossible to construct a consensus view of its argument. As the sociologist Bryan S. Turner* comments, "The Protestant ethic argument has been a topic of endless and continuous evaluation."[8] However, we cannot doubt that Weber's *The Protestant Ethic* remains a classic.

Interaction

As the British sociologist Anthony Giddens* comments, *The Protestant Ethic* was "written with polemical intent ... and is directed against economic determinism."* For Giddens,"It seems clear that Weber has Marxism in mind here, or at least the cruder forms of historical analysis which were prominent."[9] Weber's account of how religious ideas can determine the economic development of a society challenged Marxist economists and political theorists of his time. In demonstrating that ideas also have important power to cause events, Weber undermines the idea that material conditions determine the economic and class structure of society. As such, only contemporary thinkers who embrace Marxism as it was when Weber wrote *The Protestant Ethic* remain significantly challenged by the work.

Nevertheless, *The Protestant Ethic* still sparks debate. Scholars continue to publish challenges to Weber's thesis. But these challenges do not emerge from a theoretical or ideological clash. Instead, their writers wish to demonstrate whether or not the "Weber thesis," one of the most controversial arguments of the twentieth century, holds true. For example, Davide Cantoni* has argued against Weber's thesis,[10] while Leonard Dudley* and Ulrich Blum,* have argued for it.[11]

The Continuing Debate

Today, most of the debates about *The Protestant Ethic* focus less on its relevance to grand sociological theories, than on applying it to different subfields of sociology. Only a select group of Weber specialists still debate its original content or meaning.[12] The majority of scholars referring to it today use the work as a source of ideas for new research in related topics.

Nonetheless, some discussion of its content continues. Perhaps the most notable topic focuses on how Weber's thesis relates to the development of Western rationalization* and capitalism.[13] Contemporary scholars of comparative politics and political cultures such as Ronald Inglehart* and Anglo American political sociologist Pippa Norris* have written influential evaluations of Weber's argument that societies become more secular* as they become more rationalized.[14]

The discipline of sociology constantly revisits the concerns and approaches of its founders, and Weber continues to be one of the most influential sociologists. A new English translation of the 1920 edition of *The Protestant Ethic* appeared in 2001. This new edition standardized Weber's terminology and restored his original italicization, bringing out the nuance and subtlety of Weber's arguments.[15] The *Journal of Classical Sociology* frequently publishes material on Weber. So does the journal *Max Weber Studies*, which remains exclusively dedicated to debating Weber's work. These publications often address key topics around *The Protestant Ethic*.

1 Peter Hamilton, ed., *Max Weber, Critical Assessments*, vol. 1. (London: Routledge, 1991), 308.

2 Hamilton, *Max Weber, Critical Assessments*, 308.

3 Francis Fukuyama, "The Calvinist Manifesto," *The New York Times*, March 13, 2005, accessed October 18, 2015, http://www.nytimes. com/2005/03/13/books/review/the-calvinist-manifesto.html.

4 Fukuyama, "The Calvinist Manifesto."

5 Fukuyama, "The Calvinist Manifesto."

6 Fukuyama, "The Calvinist Manifesto."

7 Fukuyama, "The Calvinist Manifesto."

8 Bryan S. Turner, *Max Weber: From History to Modernity* (New York: Routledge, 2002), 25.

9 Max Weber, *The Protestant Ethic and the Spirit of Capitalism: and other writings* (London and New York: Routledge, 2005), xviii.

10 Davide Cantoni, "The Economic Effects of the Protestant Reformation: Testing the Weber Hypothesis in the German Lands," *Journal of the European Economic Association* 13, no. 4 (2014): 561–98.

11 Ulrich Blum and Leonard Dudley, "Religion and Economic Growth: Was Weber Right?" *Journal of Evolutionary Economics* 11, no. 2 (2001): 207–30.

12 Richard Swedberg, *Max Weber and the Idea of Economic Sociology* (Princeton, NJ: Princeton University Press, 2000); Peter Ghosh, *Max Weber and 'The Protestant Ethic': Twin Histories* (Oxford: Oxford University Press, 2014).

13 Nicholas Gane, *Max Weber and Postmodern Theory: Rationalization versus Re-enchantment* (Basingstoke: Palgrave, 2002).

14 Pippa Norris and Ronald Inglehart, *Sacred and Secular: Religion and Politics Worldwide* (Cambridge: Cambridge University Press, 2011).

15 Max Weber, *The Protestant Ethic and the Spirit of Capitalism: With Other Writings on the Rise of the West*, trans. Stephen Kalberg, 4th ed. (New York: Oxford University Press, 2009).

MODULE 12
WHERE NEXT?

KEY POINTS

* *The Protestant Ethic* is likely to remain an important piece of work for many years to come.

* As capitalism* continues to evolve, the arguments in *The Protestant Ethic* concerning the development of Western capitalism and the process of rationalization* will remain relevant.

* *The Protestant Ethic* played a seminal role in establishing the discipline of sociology.*

Potential

Scholars will likely consider Max Weber's *The Protestant Ethic and the Spirit of Capitalism* a classic for a long time to come. Sociologists have been drawing on it for over a hundred years now, and this seems unlikely to change.[1] Weber remains an important figure in the discipline—and *The Protestant Ethic* is one reason why. Scholars in the subfield of general social theory have long discussed Weber. Their debate remains strong, even if their discipline has been slower to grow than other fields. But scholars in a number of growing subfields, such as economic sociology* (the study of the ways in which economics are embedded in social behavior) and cultural sociology* (the study of social structures and symbols as they are understood to form culture) have also taken to citing *The Protestant Ethic* in their work.

Many contemporary sociologists find themselves addressing problems similar to those Weber discussed a century ago. And many of the responses the early sociologists offered remain relevant today. This continuing relevance distinguishes sociology from other social sciences, and makes the founding figures of the discipline particularly important. In other words, sociologists do not necessarily find *The Protestant Ethic* important as an accurate piece of empirical* scholarship. Instead, they remain attracted by its creative potential: the questions it poses and the hypotheses it allows scholars to raise. Today Weber's essay typically serves as a catalyst for related projects. It can spark debate about things like the role of culture and values in the development of the economy. It can be used to draw cross-cultural comparisons between societies. And it can aid discussions around the development of modernity and rationality.

> *"Sociology … is a science concerning itself with the interpretive understanding of social action and thereby with a causal explanation of its course and consequences."*
>
> Max Weber, *Economy and Society*

Future Directions

As a foundational work in the discipline of sociology, *The Protestant Ethic* has given rise to an incalculable amount of scholarship. More than a century after its publication, scholars have already developed every well-defined position possible. Weber felt that history had no "iron laws,"[2] seeing the "task of social theory" to facilitate "the search for historical truths."[3] Weber rejected the

Marxist* idea that academic inquiry should change society.[4] So Weberian scholars are not charged to search for any particular truth. Rather, they look to discover the truth through fair and reasonable inquiry. If Weber created followers, he wanted them to be scholars empowered to pursue their own lines of inquiry. This makes it difficult to identify any scholars in particular as Weber's heirs.

Furthermore, generations of scholars have cast considerable doubt on just about all of Weber's substantive arguments. Yes, influential thinkers such as American political scientist Francis Fukuyama* have argued for the continued importance of Weber's general claims about the influence of religion and culture on economic behavior.[5] But the British sociologist Anthony Giddens* suggests that we may question the detail of almost all of Weber's arguments: "I don't think Weber's view of methodological individualism has really stood up to the test of time ... And his theory of bureaucracy* turns out to be quite time bound ... And of course it is not proven that Protestantism* or Puritanism* were at the origins of modern capitalism, as Weber claimed."[6]

With question marks attached to Weber's main claims, few scholars remain willing to move these ideas forward.

Summary

In *The Protestant Ethic*, Max Weber claimed that the methodical conduct of life in search of profit served as an important force in the development of modern capitalism. And he believed that Protestant theology* inspired that profit-seeking motive. This argument, which has attracted much attention since its publication, has come to be known as the "Weber thesis."A relatively brief text, *The Protestant Ethic* addressed important problems contemporary with the birth of sociology as a discipline. Weber's followers in various schools would canonize these problems as fundamental sociological concerns and avenues of inquiry. For instance, we can trace scholarly interest in the origins and future of modern capitalism and Western rationalism* to Weber, as well as interest in the causal force of beliefs, values, tradition, and nonmaterial interests.

Weber claimed that religious ideas could cause economic change. This set him apart from early strongly "materialist"* interpretations of Marxist philosophy. For a while, scholars saw this as the core of Weber's originality. But today many scholars seek to synthesize Weber and Karl Marx,* interpreting Marx as less materialist and Weber as less focused on the role of ideas. In addition, the text contains a number of ambiguities, particularly regarding key concepts such as "elective affinities."* Partly this may be due to the 15-year period between its initial publication as an essay and its release in book form, with some key additions by Weber. In any event, Weber left room for multiple interpretations and over the years they have sparked much debate.

Ideas in *The Protestant Ethic* have sparked the creation of new hypotheses. Even some of its less central concepts—the "disenchantment of the world"* or the "iron cage,"* for example— have become classic sociological concepts in their own right. And scholars have come to regard many of Weber's other works as classics too. For decades, sociologists have almost unanimously considered him a founder of the discipline, alongside Karl Marx and Émile Durkheim.*

As they value other great works by the founders of sociology, scholars will continue to value *The Protestant Ethic* for a long time. Many contemporary sociological research programs and theories have grown from the problems it raises and responses great thinkers have had to them. Indeed, these responses have largely defined the discipline of sociology. Anyone interested in sociology will find inspiration in Weber's work in general and *The Protestant Ethic* in particular.

---

1 Kieran Allen, *Max Weber: A Critical Introduction* (Pluto Press, 2004), 32.

2 Guenther Roth and Wolfgang Schluchter, *Max Weber's Vision of History: Ethics and Methods* (Berkeley, CA: University of California Press, 1984), 201.

3 Ken Morrison, *Marx, Durkheim, Weber: Formations of Modern Social Thought* (London: Sage, 2006), 276.

4 Morrison, *Marx, Durkheim, Weber*, 276.

5 Francis Fukuyama, "The Calvinist Manifesto," *The New York Times*, March 13, 2005, accessed October 18, 2015, http://www.nytimes. com/2005/03/13/books/review/the-calvinist-manifesto.html.

6 Anthony Giddens and Christopher Pierson, *Conversations with Anthony Giddens: Making Sense of Modernity* (Stanford, CA: Stanford University Press, 1998), 60–1.

GLOSSARY OF TERMS

1. **Ancient Rome:** a civilization that began in the eighth century B.C.E. One of the biggest and most significant empires in the ancient world, it lasted until the fifth century C.E.

2. **Anthropology:** the study of humankind. This can often involve comparative studies of different cultures and investigating how different social structures have evolved.

3. *Archiv für Sozialwissenschaften und Sozialpolitik* **(Archive for Social Science and Social Policy):** a journal edited by Weber, Werner Sombart, and Edgar Jaffé. It was the leading German academic journal of the time.

4. **Asceticism:** Weber used the term to refer to the self-denial of pleasure. He suggested that in modern capitalism self-control and self-denial became a form of social action that created a disciplined approach to work.This asceticism had religious roots. But Weber claimed that by the nineteenth century, asceticism had become part of everyday life.

5. **Baptists:** a group within the Protestant branch of philosophy who believe that baptisms should only be performed on believers. So they oppose the common practice of baptizing infants.They also believe that baptism must involve the full immersion of the person being baptized under water.

6. **Buddhism:** a movement concerned with the spiritual development of the individual. Buddhists do not believe in a creator or personal God, but do believe that to reach nirvana—a transcendent state—people must follow the path of the Buddha.Today there are nearly 400 million Buddhists worldwide.

7. **Bureaucracy:** Weber used the term to refer to a particular type of administrative structure, associated with the process of rationalization. For example, it involved a hierarchical structure with members being selected on the basis of merit rather than social ties.

8. **Calling:** having a "calling" implied that one's work was a God-given task. The sixteenth-century German theologian Martin Luther advanced this notion.

9. **Calvinism:** A branch of Protestantism associated with the French cleric and reformer John Calvin. Calvinism emphasizes the rule of God over all things. In its earliest form, it taught predestination (the concept that some people

were destined for heaven and others were not, despite the good works they might do during their lifetimes).

10. **Capitalism:** in Weber's definition, this is an economic and social system that existed in most civilizations when economic enterprise began to calculate expected profit both before an enterprise had been undertaken and again at the end of the project. The differences would then be compared for all possible transactions. "Modern capitalism" or "Western capitalism" is a more specific organization of the economy that emerged in Western Europe and the United States. In modern capitalism, free labor is organized in a rational—calculated—manner, and the "spirit of capitalism" guides society in the systematic pursuit of profit. A more general understanding of capitalism is a system where private individuals own capital and the means of production are not collectively owned.

11. **Common law:** a law that, instead of being made by statute, is developed by judges. The decisions made by judges in individual cases serve as precedents in the law, meaning past decisions bind the future decisions of judges.

12. **Communicative action:** a term the German philosopher Jürgen Habermas used to describe action based on deliberation and argument undertaken by groups of individuals.

13. **Confucianism:** a way of life based on the teachings of Confucius, a Chinese philosopher whose life spanned the fifth and sixth centuries B.C.E.

14. **Cultural sociology:** the study of the social behavior and symbols as they are understood to constitute "culture."

15. **Culturalism:** a concept that emphasizes the importance of culture in determining social behavior.

16. **Deliberative democracy:** a form of democracy in which public deliberation is the basis of legitimate decision-making.

17. **Diaspora:** a dispersed group of people. It most often describes people forced to leave their homeland, but can be used for voluntary migration.

18. **Disenchantment of the world:** a phrase used by Weber to indicate the

process by which magic ceases to have a role in mediating humans' relation to the world. Protestantism (especially Calvinism) played a role in this disenchantment by disavowing the Roman Catholic belief that the Church could help save people's souls.

19. **Economic determinism:** the idea that economic relationships are fundamental to explaining social phenomena. This idea remains most associated with the work of Karl Marx.

20. **Economic sociology:** the study of the social causes of economic institutions and behaviors. The label was first used in the late nineteenth century. *The Protestant Ethic* is considered to be one of the most important works in economic sociology.

21. **Economic traditionalism:** a culture or economic ethic that views work as a necessary evil, less valuable than leisure, which should be performed only as required to satisfy "traditional needs."

22. **Elective affinity/inner affinity:** a somewhat ambiguous term that recurs in Weber's work, this has been the subject of some debate. It denotes a relationship between two phenomena connected by a common feature or a historical link, but which cannot be clearly demonstrated to have a causal link. Thus, Protestant beliefs did not "cause" the spirit of capitalism, but they are highly compatible with it.

23. **Empirical:** a term used to describe knowledge derived from the process of observation and experiment. We gather empirical knowledge by means of the senses.

24. **Epistemology:** a branch of philosophy concerned with the study of knowledge.

25. **Eurocentrism:** viewing the world from a purely European perspective. It generally involves a belief that European culture is superior to other cultures.

26. **Eurozone:** the collective term for all of the countries that use the euro as their currency. The eurozone includes countries such as Germany, France, and Spain.

27. **Feudalism:** a medieval social system in which status and authority were

closely bound up with land ownership and labor.

28. **Functionalism:** a theoretical approach that, inspired by biology, looks at society as a whole body composed of parts that contribute different functions to sustain it. The concept has its roots in the French philosopher Auguste Comte and the British philosopher Herbert Spencer. Émile Durkheim became the first sociologist to employ functionalist thought. Weber's translator Talcott Parsons and his follower American sociologist Robert K. Merton further elaborated the theory, making it the dominant perspective in the 1940s and 1950s.

29. **Habilitation thesis or *Habilitationsschrift*:** a professorial thesis required for habilitation, the highest academic degree—beyond even a PhD—in some European and Asian countries.

30. **Heidelberg University:** founded in 1386, it is the oldest university in Germany. It has a historic reputation for independent thought and democratic values.

31. **Hinduism:** a religion with over 900 million followers worldwide, mainly in India and Nepal. It is one of the world's oldest religions, dating back thousands of years.

32. **Historical materialism:** Karl Marx's materialist conception of history explains historical change in ideas, or the ideological superstructure, as a consequence rather than the cause of changes in the economic infrastructure.

33. **Humanities:** academic disciplines that study human culture. They include history, literature, and philosophy.

34. **Idealism:** the term used to describe the philosophical viewpoint that reality is a mental phenomenon. As such, human behavior has to be understood through interpretation of social values and cannot be reduced to material interests.

35. **Industrial Revolution:** the term used to describe the period of economic transformation via the adoption of new manufacturing processes that started in the United Kingdom in the mid-eighteenth century and then spread to Western Europe over the next one hundred years.

36. **Interpretative sociology or sociology of understanding (*verstehen*):** a sociological approach developed notably by Weber and Georg Simmel,

it focused not on describing facts, but on explaining the causes and consequences of actions by understanding their subjective *meaning*.

37. **Iron cage:** Weber concluded, metaphorically, that humans do not control their concern for material goods any more. The desire has turned into a "steel-hard casing." The first English translator of *The Protestant Ethic*, Talcott Parsons, rendered the term as "iron cage." His metaphor has become a classic concept associated with this work.

38. **Judaism:** one of the oldest world religions, dating back 3500 years. Jews believe that as God's chosen people they should endeavor to live a holy and ethical life.

39. **Lutheranism:** the name given to a branch of Protestantism that follows the theology of Martin Luther. One of the main tenets of Lutheranism is that scripture is the final authority on all religious matters.

40. **Methodism:** a religious movement begun in the eighteenth century that originally sought to reform the Church of England. Just before the end of the eighteenth century, however, it established itself as an autonomous Church.

41. **Middle Ages:** a period of European history lasting from the fifth century to the fifteenth. It is considered the middle period of history, coming after the early period of antiquity and before the modern period.

42. **Neo-Kantianism:** a branch of philosophy deeply influenced by the work of eighteenth-century German philosopher Immanuel Kant. It was Germany's leading philosophical movement between the 1870s and World War I.

43. **Pietism:** a reform movement among Lutherans in the seventeenth century. It emphasized the importance of personal faith above all else.

44. **Philology:** the study of language and languages, involving a combination of literary criticism, history, and linguistics.

45. **Positivism:** a branch of the philosophy of science and epistemology founded by the nineteenth-century French philosopher Auguste Comte, who coined the term "sociology." Positivism claims that the only valid knowledge is that which can be expressed as laws verified by experience. Positivism became

most influential through the work of one of the fathers of sociology, Émile Durkheim.

46. **Predestination:** the belief that the fate of the individual's soul has been decided by God and will arrive regardless of the individual's behavior. The term is also used to refer to other events ordained by God.

47. **Premodern:** the period up until the fifteenth century. Scholars usually characterize it as a period in which tradition and religion dominated social life.

48. **Progressive Christianity:** a theological movement common to all Christian denominations, it links Christianity with progressive concerns such as social justice.

49. **Protestantism:** a form of Christianity. It emerged following the Reformation and the split with Roman Catholicism.

50. **Prussia:** a historic state that existed between 1525 and 1947 in what is now northern Germany and parts of Poland.

51. **Puritanism:** For Weber, Puritanism involved self-denial of pleasure and a distancing of oneself from the world. Protestant sects such as Calvinism encouraged this type of behavior. Puritanism aimed to remove the Roman Catholic influence on Protestant worship.

52. **Quakers:** the term commonly used for members of the religious group the Society of Friends. The movement, which began in the mid-seventeenth century, stresses the importance of living according to one's direct knowledge of God's will.

53. **Rational accounting:** the term Weber uses to describe the process of estimating profit and loss before transactions are undertaken, as well as after they have taken place.

54. **Rational(ism):** Weber used this term to refer to both types of societies and types of behavior. A rational society used rational legal standards, rational accounting methods and exhibited a general mastery of nature. Rational behaviors are actions precisely calculated to achieve a given end.

55. **Rationalization:** a key concept in Weber's account of history and how

societies developed. Rationalization involved social life being determined to a greater and greater degree by calculation and rational behavior.

56. **Reformation:** a movement that began in the sixteenth century to reform the Roman Catholic Church. The Protestant denominations emerged in Western Europe as a result of the Reformation. The process was led notably by theologians Martin Luther in Germany and John Calvin in France, among others.

57. **Roman Catholicism:** a tradition within the Christian Church that dates back 2000 years. It is the largest of all the Christian religious traditions with over 1.2 billion followers worldwide.

58. **Sects:** religious groups. Unlike Churches, they admit only members who fulfill certain criteria. Membership implies submitting to the group's monitoring of one's good character.

59. **Secular:** refers to something separate from religious institutions and religious beliefs. For example, secular education is not directed by religious teaching or undertaken by religious institutions.

60. **Sociology:** the academic study of the way humans behave. This can involve behavior from the individual level to the whole of society. Sociology seeks to explain this behavior by examining the origins of social human behavior, the way it is organized, and how humans behave under different systems of rules.

61. **Sociology of organizations:** the study of formal and informal institutions. It focuses on how these institutions are structured and the way they determine individuals' behavior.

62. **"Spirit of capitalism":** Weber used this phrase to refer to the systematic organization of life around money, profit, work, competition, and material success as ends in themselves. The "spirit of capitalism," according to Weber, came about following Calvin's teachings on salvation. Calvin emphasized personal self-control, which then extended to self-control in one's economic behavior.

63. **Structuration theory:** developed by the sociologist Anthony Giddens. It holds that while social life is more than the sum of individual acts, it is

not just determined by social forces. Because people interact with social structures, structures such as traditions can be changed over time.

64. **Taoism:** a Chinese tradition of philosophy and religious belief. Taoism is concerned with following the Tao, translated as "the way." The substance of the Tao is difficult to define, but it is best understood as the creative principle of the universe.

65. **Theology:** a term that can be used to refer to the study of religious ideas. It can also be used as a collective term for specific religious ideas and concepts collectively, e.g., Protestant theology.

66. **Unitarianism:** a theology characterized by understanding God as one being—against the more common Christian interpretation of God as a Trinity, simultaneously Father, Son, and Holy Spirit.

67. **University of Freiburg:** founded in 1457, it is the fifth-oldest university in Germany, with a long tradition of education in the social and natural sciences.

68. **Utilitarianism:** a normative ethical theory that claims that a morally right act is one that maximizes utility. Utility is usually understood in terms of happiness, meaning a moral action will maximize pleasure and minimize pain.

69. ***Verein für Socialpolitik* (Social Policy Association):** an influential society of German economists founded in 1873. Its members included Max Weber and Werner Sombart.

70. **Vocation:** an ethic of work marked by the feeling of a "calling" or God-given task. While Weber searched for this type of belief among many religions, he found it only in Protestantism.

71. **World War I:** a global conflict centered in Europe between 1914 and 1918. The war involved countries such as France, Britain, Russia, and the United States on one side and Germany, Austria-Hungary, and the Ottoman Empire on the other.

1. **Arjun Appadurai (b. 1949)** is an Indian anthropologist based in the United States, one of the most influential contemporary authors in the study of modernity and globalization. His most famous book, *Modernity at Large: Cultural Dimensions of Globalization* (1996), contains various references to Weber.

2. **Sascha O. Becker (b. 1973)** is a German economist currently working at the University of Warwick. His research interests include economic history and labor economics.

3. **Reinhard Bendix (1916−91)** was a German sociologist who immigrated to the United States. His most influential work was *Max Weber: An Intellectual Portrait* (1960).

4. **James Blaut (1927−2000)**, a professor of anthropology and geography at the University of Illinois, was one of the foremost critics of Eurocentrism.

5. **Ulrich Blum (b. 1953)** is a German economist at Martin Luther University of Halle-Wittenberg in Germany. His research interests include institutional economics and industrial economics.

6. **Luc Boltanski (b. 1940)** is a leading figure in the French school of "pragmatic sociology." His most famous work is *The New Spirit of Capitalism* (1999), coauthored with Ève Chiapello.

7. **Pierre Bourdieu (1930−2002)** was an important French sociologist and philosopher, most famous for his books *Distinction: A Social Critique of the Judgment of Taste* (1984) and *Outline of a Theory of Practice* (1977). Both of these works have been translated into English by Richard Nice.

8. **Lujo Brentano (1844−1931)** was a German economist and contemporary of Weber. Weber engages most notably with his book *The Beginnings of Modern Capitalism* (1916).

9. **John Calvin (1509−64)** was a French theologian and influential figure during the Protestant Reformation. He became associated with a branch of Protestantism called Calvinism, which held that all individuals are predestined by God to achieve either salvation or damnation.

10. **Davide Cantoni (b. 1981)** is an Italian German economist at the Ludwig

Maximilian University of Munich. His research interests include economic history and political economy.

11. **Ève Chiapello (b. 1965)** is a French professor of management, best known for coauthoring *The New Spirit of Capitalism* (1999).

12. **Ralf Dahrendorf (1929–2009)** was a German British sociologist and politician, most influential for his development of conflict theory in *Class and Class Conflict in Industrial Society* (1957).

13. **Wilhelm Dilthey (1833–1911)** was a German philosopher best known for his *Introduction to the Human Sciences:An Attempt to Lay a Foundation for the Study of Society and History* (1923).

14. **Leonard Dudley (b. 1943)** is a Canadian economist working at the University of Montreal. His research interests include the effect of information technology on economic growth and political institutions.

15. **Émile Durkheim (1858–1917)** was a French sociologist most famous for his books *The Elementary Forms of Religious Life* (1912), *Suicide* (1897), and *The Division of Labour in Society* (1893).

16. **H. Karl Fischer** has not been clearly identified. Many Karl Fischers worked in German academia in Weber's day and he has no famous works other than the debate with Weber. It seems most likely that he was a scholar of German history born in 1840.

17. **Benjamin Franklin (1706–90)** was one of the Founding Fathers of the United States. Aside from being a politician he was a scientist, a printer, a diplomat, an inventor, and an author.

18. **Francis Fukuyama (b. 1952)** is an American political scientist and theorist. His best-known work is *The End of History and the Last Man* (1992) in which he controversially argued that following the fall of the Soviet Union, liberal capitalism had become the final form of human government.

19. **Peter Ghosh** is a British historian at the University of Oxford. His research interests include the interface between English politics and political ideas in the nineteenth century, and Max Weber.

20. **Anthony Giddens (b. 1938)** is an influential British sociologist best known for his *The Constitution of Society: Outline of the Theory of Structuration* (1984). Scholars consider Giddens to be one of the most important modern sociologists—if not *the* most important. He is the fifth most-referenced author in the humanities.

21. **Eberhard Gothein (1853–1923)** was a historian of culture and economics and a strong supporter of the foundation of the German Society for Sociology. He is most famous for his *Economic History of the Black Forest* (1892).

22. **Alvin W. Gouldner (1920–80)** was an important Marxist sociologist in the United States, most famous for his books *The Coming Crisis of Western Sociology* (1970) and *Patterns of Industrial Bureaucracy* (1954). The latter work applies Weberian concepts to the study of industrial relations.

23. **Jürgen Habermas (b. 1929)** is an influential German sociologist and philosopher, most famous for his *Theory of Communicative Action* (1981), which contains a full section on *The Protestant Ethic.*

24. **Ronald Inglehart (b. 1934)** is an influential political scientist in the United States, most famous for his book *Modernization and Postmodernization: Cultural, Economic, and Political Change in 43 Societies* (1997).

25. **Edgar Jaffé (1861–1921)** was a student of Max Weber and Werner Sombart, and an editor of the *Archive for the Social Sciences and Social Policy.* Jaffé's scholarly work focused on the workings of the English economy.

26. **Georg Jellinek (1851–1911)** was an Austrian lawyer and philosopher of law, best known for *The Declaration of the Rights of Man and Citizens* (1895), which inspired him to study the social consequences of Puritanism.

27. **Martin Luther (1483–1546)** was a German theologian whose writings helped inspire the Protestant Reformation. In 1534, he published a complete translation of the Bible in German, believing that people should be able to read it in their own language. Lutheranism is a branch of Protestantism that identifies with the theology of Martin Luther.

28. **Karl Marx (1818–83)** was a German philosopher, journalist, economist, sociologist, and revolutionary, most famous for writing *The Communist*

Manifesto (1848)—with Friedrich Engels—and *Das Kapital* (1867–94).

29. **Charles Wright Mills (1916–62)**, one of the most influential mid-twentieth-century sociologists in the United States, was most famous for writing *The Power Elite* (1956) and *The Sociological Imagination* (1959). With the sociologist Hans H. Gerth he cotranslated selections of Weber's writing, published as *From Max Weber* (1948). This book played a key role in making Weber available to the English-speaking world.

30. **Pippa Norris (b. 1953)** is a political scientist based at Harvard University. Her research interests include gender politics and the barriers women face in politics, as well as the relevance and roots of political culture.

31. **Talcott Parsons (1902–79)** was one of the most influential sociologists in the United States and parts of Europe in the mid-twentieth century. He received his PhD from Heidelberg, where he studied with Max Weber's friend the philosopher Karl Jaspers, his brother Alfred Weber, and the classical sociologist Karl Mannheim. Other than his 1930 translation of *The Protestant Ethic*, his most famous work is *The Social System* (1951).

32. **Sir William Petty (1623–87)** was a British political economist who wrote about the role of the state in the economy. In addition to his economic work he was a qualified doctor, a professor of music, and a member of the British Parliament.

33. **Felix Rachfahl (1867–1925)** was a historian of German and Dutch history, mostly known for his discussion with Weber about *The Protestant Ethic and the Spirit of Capitalism*.

34. **Heinrich Rickert (1863–1936)** was a leading figure of the Baden school of neo-Kantian philosophy and a friend of Weber. He is best known for writing *The Limits of Concept Formation in Natural Science: A Logical Introduction to the Historical Sciences* (1896 and 1902).

35. **Wolfgang Schluchter (b. 1938)** is a leading figure among German Weberian sociologists and editor of Max Weber's complete works in German. He is best known for his book *The Rise of Western Rationalism: Max Weber's Developmental History* (1979).

36. **Georg Simmel (1858–1918)**, a philosopher and sociologist, ranks among the most important classical sociologists.With Weber, he cofounded the German Society for Sociology. His most influential works are *The Metropolis and Mental Life* (1903) and *The Philosophy of Money* (1907).

37. **Werner Sombart (1863–1941)** was a Marxist economist and sociologist. He is famous in English-language sociology not only for his controversy with Weber on modern capitalism, but also for his book *Why Is There No Socialism in the United States?* (1906).This seminal work deals with American exceptionalism—the idea that the United States believes it differs from other industrialized countries, especially in its politics.

38. **Richard Swedberg (b. 1948)** is a Swedish sociologist working in the United States. One of his best-known works is *Max Weber and the Idea of Economic Sociology* (2000).

39. **Alexis de Tocqueville (1805–59)** was a French political theorist and historian. He is best known for his two-volume study of American society *Democracy in America* (1835 and 1840).

40. **Ernst Troeltsch (1865–1923)** was a theologian, best known for his book *The Social Teaching of the Christian Churches* (1911), which Weber described as a confirmation and supplement to his essay.

41. **Bryan S.Turner (b. 1945)** is a British Australian sociologist most famous for writing *The Body and Society: Explorations in Social Theory* (1984). He is also coauthor of *Max Weber on Economy and Society* and the editor of the *Journal of Classical Sociology*, which frequently publishes new work about Weber.

42. **Marianne Weber (1870–1954)** a sociologist and women's rights activist who married Max Weber. She posthumously published her husband's unpublished work, including his magnum opus *Economy and Society*, and she wrote the authoritative *Max Weber:A Biography* (1926).

43. **Wilhelm Windelband (1848–1915)**, another leading figure of the Badenschool of neo-Kantian philosophy, was most famous for his 1893 work *A History of Philosophy*.

44. **Ludger Woessmann** is a German economist working at the University of Munich. His research interests included the determinants of long-run prosperity and the determinants of student achievement.

 **WORKS CITED**

1. Allen, Kieran. *Max Weber: A Critical Introduction*. London: Pluto Press, 2004.

2. Arnot, Chris. "Protestant v Catholic: Which Countries Are More Successful?" *Guardian*, October 31, 2011. Accessed September 5, 2015. http://www. theguardian.com/education/2011/oct/31/economics-religion-research.

3. Baehr, Peter. "The 'Iron Cage' and the 'Shell as Hard as Steel': Parsons, Weber, and the Stahlhartes Gehäuse Metaphor in the Protestant Ethic and the Spirit of Capitalism." *History and Theory* 40, no. 2 (2001): 153–69.

4. Barker, James R. "Tightening the Iron Cage: Concertive Control in Self-Managing Teams." *Administrative Science Quarterly* 38, no. 3 (1993): 408–37.

5. Becker, Sascha O., and Ludger Wohmann. "Was Weber Wrong? A Human Capital Theory of Protestant Economic History." Program on Education Policy and Governance, Harvard University (2007).

6. Bell, Daniel. "The Protestant Ethic." *World Policy Journal* 13, no. 3 (1996): 35–9. Blaut, J. M. *Eight Eurocentric Historians*. New York: Guilford Press, 2000.

7. Blum, Ulrich, and Leonard Dudley. "Religion and Economic Growth: Was Weber Right?" *Journal of Evolutionary Economics* 11, no. 2 (2001): 207–30.

8. Boltanski, Luc, and Eve Chiapello. "The New Spirit of Capitalism." *International Journal of Politics, Culture, and Society* 18, no. 3–4 (2005): 161–88.

9. Cantoni, Davide. "The Economic Effects of the Protestant Reformation: Testing the Weber Hypothesis in the German Lands." *Journal of the European Economic Association* 13, no. 4 (2014): 561–98.

10. Dillon, Michele. *Introduction to Sociological Theory: Theorists, Concepts, and Their Applicability to the Twenty-First Century*. Chichester: John Wiley & Sons, 2009.

11. Edles, Laura Desfor, and Scott Appelrouth. *Sociological Theory in the Classical Era: Text and Readings*. Third edition. Thousand Oaks, CA: Sage, 2014.

12. Fukuyama, Francis. "The Calvinist Manifesto." *The New York Times*, March 13, 2005. Accessed October 18, 2015. http://www.nytimes.com/2005/03/13/books/review/the-calvinist-manifesto.html.

13. Gane, Nicholas. *Max Weber and Postmodern Theory: Rationalization versus Re-enchantment*. Basingstoke: Palgrave, 2002.

14. Ghosh, Peter. *Max Weber and 'The Protestant Ethic': Twin Histories*. Oxford: Oxford University Press, 2014.

15. Giddens, Anthony, and Christopher Pierson. *Conversations with Anthony Giddens: Making Sense of Modernity*. Stanford, CA: Stanford University Press, 1998.

16. Gouldner, Alvin W. *Patterns of Industrial Bureaucracy*. Glencoe, IL: Free Press, 1954.

17. Hamilton, Peter, ed. *Max Weber, Critical Assessments*. Vol. 1. London: Routledge, 1991.

18. Harrison, Lawrence E., and Samuel P. Huntington. *Culture Matters: How Values Shape Human Progress*. New York: Basic Books, 2000.

19. Inglehart, Ronald. *Modernization and Postmodernization: Cultural, Economic, and Political Change in 43 Societies*. Princeton, NJ: Princeton University Press, 1997.

20. Lehmann, Hartmut, and Guenther Roth. *Weber's Protestant Ethic: Origins, Evidence, Contexts*. Cambridge: Cambridge University Press, 1995.

21. MacIntyre, Alasdair (1984) *After Virtue: A Study in Moral Theory*. Second edition. Notre Dame, IN: University of Notre Dame Press.

22. McCormick, John P. *Weber, Habermas and Transformations of the European State: Constitutional, Social, and Supranational Democracy*. Cambridge: Cambridge University Press, 2007.

23. Mills, C. Wright. *White Collar: The American Middle Classes*. Oxford: Oxford University Press, 2002.

24. Morrison, Ken. *Marx, Durkheim, Weber: Formations of Modern Social Thought*. London: Sage, 2006.

25. Nee, Victor and Richard Swedburg, *On Capitalism*. Stanford, CA: Stanford University Press, 2007.

26. Norris, Pippa, and Ronald Inglehart. *Sacred and Secular: Religion and Politics Worldwide*. Cambridge: Cambridge University Press, 2011.

27. Ransome, Paul. *Social Theory for Beginners*. Bristol: Policy, 2010.

28. Ringer, Fritz. *Max Weber: An Intellectual Biography*. Chicago: University of Chicago Press, 2010.

29. Roth, Guenther and Wolfgang Schluchter. *Max Weber's Vision of History: Ethics and Methods*. Berkeley, CA: University of California Press (1984).

30. Schafer, D. Paul. *Revolution or Renaissance: Making the Transition from an Economic Age to a Cultural Age*. Ottawa: University of Ottawa Press, 2008.

31. Sombart, Werner. *Der moderne Kapitalismus: Bd. Die Genesis des Kapitalismus*. Vol. 1. Leipzig: Duncker & Humblot, 1902.

32. *The Jews and Modern Capitalism*. Kitchener, ON: Batoche Books, 2001.

33. Swedberg, Richard. "The Economic Sociologies of Pierre Bourdieu." *Cultural Sociology* 5, no. 1 (2011): 67–82.

34. *Max Weber and the Idea of Economic Sociology*. Princeton, NJ: Princeton University Press, 2000.

35. Tenbruck, Friedrich H. "The Problem of Thematic Unity in the Works of Max Weber." *British Journal of Sociology* 31, no. 3 (1980): 316–51.

36. Turner, Bryan S. *Max Weber: From History to Modernity*. New York: Routledge, 2002.

37. Turner, Stephen P. *The Cambridge Companion to Weber*. Cambridge: Cambridge University Press, 2000.

38. Weber, Marianne. *Max Weber: A Biography*. Translated and edited by Harry Zohn. New Brunswick, NJ: Transaction Publishers, 1988.

39. Weber, Max. *Economy and Society: An Outline of Interpretive Sociology*. Edited by Guenther Roth and Claus Wittich. Berkeley, CA: University of California Press, 1978.

40. *The Protestant Ethic and the Spirit of Capitalism*. Translated by Talcott Parsons. London: Routledge, 2005.

41. *The Protestant Ethic and the "Spirit" of Capitalism: And Other Writings*. Translated by Peter Baehr and Gordon C. Wells. New York: Penguin, 2002.

42. *The Protestant Ethic and the Spirit of Capitalism: With Other Writings on the Rise of the West*. Translated by Stephen Kalberg. Fourth edition. New York: Oxford University Press, 2009.

43. "The Protestant Sects and the Spirit of Capitalism." In *The Protestant Ethic and the "Spirit" of Capitalism: And Other Writings*. Translated by Peter Baehr and Gordon C. Wells. New York: Penguin, 2002.

44. *The Religion of China: Confucianism and Taoism*. Translated by Hans H. Gerth. New York: Free Press, 1951.

45. "Science as a Vocation." *Daedalus* 87, no. 1 (1958): 111–34.

46. Whimster, Sam. *Understanding Weber*. New York: Routledge, 2007.

原书作者简介

马克斯·韦伯（Max Weber）1864 年出生于普鲁士，是德国最伟大的政治思想家之一，也是社会学奠基人之一和杰出的经济学家。他作为大学教授和编辑以富有思想而广受好评，其政治理论和思想在一战德国战败后的社会动荡中引起高度重视。他是德国民主党的创始人之一，并且参与了魏玛共和国宪法的起草设计。1920 年韦伯因患肺炎去世，年仅 56 岁。

本书作者简介

塞巴斯蒂安·古兹曼（Sebastian G. Guzman）获纽约社会研究新学院社会学博士学位，现任教于宾州西彻斯特大学，曾在《社会学理论》《社会学论坛》《古典社会学期刊》上发表多篇论文。

詹姆斯·希尔（James Hill），伦敦国王学院政治经济学研究生。

世界名著中的批判性思维

《世界思想宝库钥匙丛书》致力于深入浅出地阐释全世界著名思想家的观点，不论是谁、在何处都能了解到，从而推进批判性思维发展。

《世界思想宝库钥匙丛书》与世界顶尖大学的一流学者合作，为一系列学科中最有影响的著作推出新的分析文本，介绍其观点和影响。在这一不断扩展的系列中，每种选入的著作都代表了历经时间考验的思想典范。通过为这些著作提供必要背景、揭示原作者的学术渊源以及说明这些著作所产生的影响，本系列图书希望让读者以新视角看待这些划时代的经典之作。读者应学会思考、运用并挑战这些著作中的观点，而不是简单接受它们。

ABOUT THE AUTHOR OF THE ORIGINAL WORK

Max Weber was born in Prussia in 1864 and is known as one of Germany's greatest political thinkers. He is also credited with helping found the discipline of sociology, and for his impressive economic work. Weber's reputation for thoughtfulness led to a career as a professor and editor, while his political knowledge and ideas were highly regarded, particularly during the turmoil that followed Germany's defeat in World War I. He co-founded the German Democratic Party and advised on the draft of the country's post-war constitution. Weber died of pneumonia in 1920, aged just 56.

ABOUT THE AUTHORS OF THE ANALYSIS

Sebastián G. Guzmán undertook his PhD research in sociology at the New School for Social Research in New York. He has taught at the Universidad Andrès Bello, Chile, and is currently Assistant Professor of Sociology at West Chester University of Pennsylvania.

James Hill did his postgraduate research in political economy at King's College London.

ABOUT MACAT
GREAT WORKS FOR CRITICAL THINKING

Macat is focused on making the ideas of the world's great thinkers accessible and comprehensible to everybody, everywhere, in ways that promote the development of enhanced critical thinking skills.

It works with leading academics from the world's top universities to produce new analyses that focus on the ideas and the impact of the most influential works ever written across a wide variety of academic disciplines. Each of the works that sit at the heart of its growing library is an enduring example of great thinking. But by setting them in context — and looking at the influences that shaped their authors, as well as the responses they provoked — Macat encourages readers to look at these classics and game-changers with fresh eyes. Readers learn to think, engage and challenge their ideas, rather than simply accepting them.

批判性思维与《新教伦理与资本主义精神》

首要批判性思维技巧：分析性思维

次要批判性思维技能：理性化思维

德国社会学家马克斯·韦伯是公认的社会学奠基人之一，20 世纪最有影响力的学者之一。他的代表作《新教伦理与资本主义精神》是社会学研究的不朽杰作，以其严谨、周密的论证而著称。

韦伯致力于考察资本主义发展与欧洲不同宗教观之间的关系。许多学者更关注资本主义兴起的物质和工具性原因，但韦伯试图证明不同的宗教信仰实际上起到了重要的作用。因此，他分析资本主义与宗教观之间的关系，认真研究新教与世俗资本主义伦理的重叠程度，以及两者在多大程度上相互反映。

韦伯研究的关键，在于他考虑文化价值在多大程度上成为强化资本主义伦理和行为的隐性原因——他所作的调查嘲弄了那些巩固资本主义的"论据"。韦伯的分析敏锐而富有洞察力，今天仍得到学者的共鸣。

CRITICAL THINKING AND *THE PROTESTANT ETHIC AND THE SPIRIT OF CAPITALISM*

- Primary critical thinking skill: ANALYSIS
- Secondary critical thinking skill: REASONING

The German sociologist Max Weber is considered to be one of the founding fathers of sociology, and ranks among the most influential writers of the 20th-century. His most famous book, *The Protestant Ethic and the Spirit of Capitalism*, is a masterpiece of sociological analysis whose power is based on the construction of a rigorous, and intricately interlinked, piece of argumentation.

Weber's object was to examine the relationship between the development of capitalism and the different religious ideologies of Europe. While many other scholars focused on the material and instrumental causes of capitalism's emergence, Weber sought to demonstrate that different religious beliefs in fact played a significant role. In order to do this, he employed his analytical skills to understand the relationship between capitalism and religious ideology, carefully considering how far Protestant and secular capitalist ethics overlapped, and to what extent they mirrored each other.

One crucial element of Weber's work was his consideration the degree to which cultural values acted as implicit or hidden reasons reinforcing capitalist ethics and behavior—an investigation that he based on teasing out the 'arguments' that underpin capitalism. Incisive and insightful, Weber's analysis continues to resonate with scholars today.

《世界思想宝库钥匙丛书》简介

　　《世界思想宝库钥匙丛书》致力于为一系列在各领域产生重大影响的人文社科类经典著作提供独特的学术探讨。每一本读物都不仅仅是原经典著作的内容摘要，而是介绍并深入研究原经典著作的学术渊源、主要观点和历史影响。这一丛书的目的是提供一套学习资料，以促进读者掌握批判性思维，从而更全面、深刻地去理解重要思想。

　　每一本读物分为 3 个部分：学术渊源、学术思想和学术影响，每个部分下有 4 个小节。这些章节旨在从各个方面研究原经典著作及其反响。

　　由于独特的体例，每一本读物不但易于阅读，而且另有一项优点：所有读物的编排体例相同，读者在进行某个知识层面的调查或研究时可交叉参阅多本该丛书中的相关读物，从而开启跨领域研究的路径。

　　为了方便阅读，每本读物最后还列出了术语表和人名表（在书中则以星号＊标记），此外还有参考文献。

　　《世界思想宝库钥匙丛书》与剑桥大学合作，理清了批判性思维的要点，即如何通过 6 种技能来进行有效思考。其中 3 种技能让我们能够理解问题，另 3 种技能让我们有能力解决问题。这 6 种技能合称为"批判性思维 PACIER 模式"，它们是：

分析：了解如何建立一个观点；
评估：研究一个观点的优点和缺点；
阐释：对意义所产生的问题加以理解；
创造性思维：提出新的见解，发现新的联系；
解决问题：提出切实有效的解决办法；
理性化思维：创建有说服力的观点。

了解更多信息，请浏览 www.macat.com。

THE MACAT LIBRARY

The Macat Library is a series of unique academic explorations of seminal works in the humanities and social sciences — books and papers that have had a significant and widely recognised impact on their disciplines. It has been created to serve as much more than just a summary of what lies between the covers of a great book. It illuminates and explores the influences on, ideas of, and impact of that book. Our goal is to offer a learning resource that encourages critical thinking and fosters a better, deeper understanding of important ideas.

Each publication is divided into three Sections: Influences, Ideas, and Impact. Each Section has four Modules. These explore every important facet of the work, and the responses to it.

This Section-Module structure makes a Macat Library book easy to use, but it has another important feature. Because each Macat book is written to the same format, it is possible (and encouraged!) to cross-reference multiple Macat books along the same lines of inquiry or research. This allows the reader to open up interesting interdisciplinary pathways.

To further aid your reading, lists of glossary terms and people mentioned are included at the end of this book (these are indicated by an asterisk [*] throughout) — as well as a list of works cited.

Macat has worked with the University of Cambridge to identify the elements of critical thinking and understand the ways in which six different skills combine to enable effective thinking.

Three allow us to fully understand a problem; three more give us the tools to solve it. Together, these six skills make up the PACIER model of critical thinking. They are:

ANALYSIS — understanding how an argument is built
EVALUATION — exploring the strengths and weaknesses of an argument
INTERPRETATION — understanding issues of meaning
CREATIVE THINKING — coming up with new ideas and fresh connections
PROBLEM-SOLVING — producing strong solutions
REASONING — creating strong arguments

To find out more, visit WWW.MACAT.COM.

"《世界思想宝库钥匙丛书》提供了独一无二的跨学科学习和研究工具。它介绍那些革新了各自学科研究的经典著作，还邀请全世界一流专家和教育机构进行严谨的分析，为每位读者打开世界顶级教育的大门。"

—— 安德烈亚斯·施莱歇尔，
经济合作与发展组织教育与技能司司长

"《世界思想宝库钥匙丛书》直面大学教育的巨大挑战……他们组建了一支精干而活跃的学者队伍，来推出在研究广度上颇具新意的教学材料。"

—— 布罗尔斯教授、勋爵，剑桥大学前校长

"《世界思想宝库钥匙丛书》的愿景令人赞叹。它通过分析和阐释那些曾深刻影响人类思想以及社会、经济发展的经典文本，提供了新的学习方法。它推动批判性思维，这对于任何社会和经济体来说都是至关重要的。这就是未来的学习方法。"

—— 查尔斯·克拉克阁下，英国前教育大臣

"对于那些影响了各自领域的著作，《世界思想宝库钥匙丛书》能让人们立即了解到围绕那些著作展开的评论性言论，这让该系列图书成为在这些领域从事研究的师生们不可或缺的资源。"

—— 威廉·特朗佐教授，加利福尼亚大学圣地亚哥分校

"Macat offers an amazing first-of-its-kind tool for interdisciplinary learning and research. Its focus on works that transformed their disciplines and its rigorous approach, drawing on the world's leading experts and educational institutions, opens up a world-class education to anyone."

—— Andreas Schleicher, Director for Education and Skills, Organisation for Economic Co-operation and Development

"Macat is taking on some of the major challenges in university education... They have drawn together a strong team of active academics who are producing teaching materials that are novel in the breadth of their approach."

—— Prof Lord Broers, former Vice-Chancellor of the University of Cambridge

"The Macat vision is exceptionally exciting. It focuses upon new modes of learning which analyse and explain seminal texts which have profoundly influenced world thinking and so social and economic development. It promotes the kind of critical thinking which is essential for any society and economy. This is the learning of the future."

—— Rt Hon Charles Clarke, former UK Secretary of State for Education

"The Macat analyses provide immediate access to the critical conversation surrounding the books that have shaped their respective discipline, which will make them an invaluable resource to all of those, students and teachers, working in the field."

—— Prof William Tronzo, University of California at San Diego

TITLE	中文书名	类别
An Analysis of Arjun Appadurai's *Modernity at Large: Cultural Dimensions of Globalisation*	解析阿尔君·阿帕杜莱《消失的现代性：全球化的文化维度》	人类学
An Analysis of Claude Lévi-Strauss's *Structural Anthropology*	解析克劳德·列维–斯特劳斯《结构人类学》	人类学
An Analysis of Marcel Mauss's *The Gift*	解析马塞尔·莫斯《礼物》	人类学
An Analysis of Jared M. Diamond's *Guns, Germs, and Steel: The Fate of Human Societies*	解析贾雷德·戴蒙德《枪炮、病菌与钢铁：人类社会的命运》	人类学
An Analysis of Clifford Geertz's *The Interpretation of Cultures*	解析克利福德·格尔茨《文化的解释》	人类学
An Analysis of Philippe Ariès's *Centuries of Childhood: A Social History of Family Life*	解析菲力浦·阿利埃斯《儿童的世纪：旧制度下的儿童和家庭生活》	人类学
An Analysis of W. Chan Kim & Renée Mauborgne's *Blue Ocean Strategy*	解析金伟灿/勒妮·莫博涅《蓝海战略》	商业
An Analysis of John P. Kotter's *Leading Change*	解析约翰·P.科特《领导变革》	商业
An Analysis of Michael E. Porter's *Competitive Strategy: Creating and Sustaining Superior Performance*	解析迈克尔·E.波特《竞争战略：分析产业和竞争对手的技术》	商业
An Analysis of Jean Lave & Etienne Wenger's *Situated Learning: Legitimate Peripheral Participation*	解析琼·莱夫/艾蒂纳·温格《情境学习：合法的边缘性参与》	商业
An Analysis of Douglas McGregor's *The Human Side of Enterprise*	解析道格拉斯·麦格雷戈《企业的人性面》	商业
An Analysis of Milton Friedman's *Capitalism and Freedom*	解析米尔顿·弗里德曼《资本主义与自由》	商业
An Analysis of Ludwig von Mises's *The Theory of Money and Credit*	解析路德维希·冯·米塞斯《货币和信用理论》	经济学
An Analysis of Adam Smith's *The Wealth of Nations*	解析亚当·斯密《国富论》	经济学
An Analysis of Thomas Piketty's *Capital in the Twenty-First Century*	解析托马斯·皮凯蒂《21世纪资本论》	经济学
An Analysis of Nassim Nicholas Taleb's *The Black Swan: The Impact of the Highly Improbable*	解析纳西姆·尼古拉斯·塔勒布《黑天鹅：如何应对不可预知的未来》	经济学
An Analysis of Ha-Joon Chang's *Kicking Away the Ladder*	解析张夏准《富国陷阱：发达国家为何踢开梯子》	经济学
An Analysis of Thomas Robert Malthus's *An Essay on the Principle of Population*	解析托马斯·马尔萨斯《人口论》	经济学

An Analysis of John Maynard Keynes's *The General Theory of Employment, Interest and Money*	解析约翰·梅纳德·凯恩斯《就业、利息和货币通论》	经济学
An Analysis of Milton Friedman's *The Role of Monetary Policy*	解析米尔顿·弗里德曼《货币政策的作用》	经济学
An Analysis of Burton G. Malkiel's *A Random Walk Down Wall Street*	解析伯顿·G.马尔基尔《漫步华尔街》	经济学
An Analysis of Friedrich A. Hayek's *The Road to Serfdom*	解析弗里德里希·A.哈耶克《通往奴役之路》	经济学
An Analysis of Charles P. Kindleberger's *Manias, Panics, and Crashes: A History of Financial Crises*	解析查尔斯·P.金德尔伯格《疯狂、惊恐和崩溃：金融危机史》	经济学
An Analysis of Amartya Sen's *Development as Freedom*	解析阿马蒂亚·森《以自由看待发展》	经济学
An Analysis of Rachel Carson's *Silent Spring*	解析蕾切尔·卡森《寂静的春天》	地理学
An Analysis of Charles Darwin's *On the Origin of Species: by Means of Natural Selection, or The Preservation of Favoured Races in the Struggle for Life*	解析查尔斯·达尔文《物种起源》	地理学
An Analysis of World Commission on Environment and Development's *The Brundtland Report, Our Common Future*	解析世界环境与发展委员会《布伦特兰报告：我们共同的未来》	地理学
An Analysis of James E. Lovelock's *Gaia: A New Look at Life on Earth*	解析詹姆斯·E.拉伍洛克《盖娅：地球生命的新视野》	地理学
An Analysis of Paul Kennedy's *The Rise and Fall of the Great Powers: Economic Change and Military Conflict from 1500—2000*	解析保罗·肯尼迪《大国的兴衰：1500—2000 年的经济变革与军事冲突》	历史
An Analysis of Janet L. Abu-Lughod's *Before European Hegemony: The World System A. D. 1250—1350*	解析珍妮特·L.阿布-卢格霍德《欧洲霸权之前：1250—1350 年的世界体系》	历史
An Analysis of Alfred W. Crosby's *The Columbian Exchange: Biological and Cultural Consequences of 1492*	解析艾尔弗雷德·W.克罗斯比《哥伦布大交换：1492 年以后的生物影响和文化冲击》	历史
An Analysis of Tony Judt's *Postwar: A History of Europe since 1945*	解析托尼·贾德《战后欧洲史》	历史
An Analysis of Richard J. Evans's *In Defence of History*	解析理查德·J.艾文斯《捍卫历史》	历史
An Analysis of Eric Hobsbawm's *The Age of Revolution: Europe 1789–1848*	解析艾瑞克·霍布斯鲍姆《革命的年代：欧洲 1789—1848 年》	历史

An Analysis of Roland Barthes's *Mythologies*	解析罗兰·巴特《神话学》	文学与批判理论
An Analysis of Simon de Beauvoir's *The Second Sex*	解析西蒙娜·德·波伏娃《第二性》	文学与批判理论
An Analysis of Edward W. Said's *Orientalism*	解析爱德华·W.萨义德《东方主义》	文学与批判理论
An Analysis of Virginia Woolf's *A Room of One's Own*	解析弗吉尼亚·伍尔芙《一间自己的房间》	文学与批判理论
An Analysis of Judith Butler's *Gender Trouble*	解析朱迪斯·巴特勒《性别麻烦》	文学与批判理论
An Analysis of Ferdinand de Saussure's *Course in General Linguistics*	解析费尔迪南·德·索绪尔《普通语言学教程》	文学与批判理论
An Analysis of Susan Sontag's *On Photography*	解析苏珊·桑塔格《论摄影》	文学与批判理论
An Analysis of Walter Benjamin's *The Work of Art in the Age of Mechanical Reproduction*	解析瓦尔特·本雅明《机械复制时代的艺术作品》	文学与批判理论
An Analysis of W.E.B. Du Bois's *The Souls of Black Folk*	解析 W.E.B. 杜波依斯《黑人的灵魂》	文学与批判理论
An Analysis of Plato's *The Republic*	解析柏拉图《理想国》	哲学
An Analysis of Plato's *Symposium*	解析柏拉图《会饮篇》	哲学
An Analysis of Aristotle's *Metaphysics*	解析亚里士多德《形而上学》	哲学
An Analysis of Aristotle's *Nicomachean Ethics*	解析亚里士多德《尼各马可伦理学》	哲学
An Analysis of Immanuel Kant's *Critique of Pure Reason*	解析伊曼努尔·康德《纯粹理性批判》	哲学
An Analysis of Ludwig Wittgenstein's *Philosophical Investigations*	解析路德维希·维特根斯坦《哲学研究》	哲学
An Analysis of G.W.F. Hegel's *Phenomenology of Spirit*	解析 G.W.F. 黑格尔《精神现象学》	哲学
An Analysis of Baruch Spinoza's *Ethics*	解析巴鲁赫·斯宾诺莎《伦理学》	哲学
An Analysis of Hannah Arendt's *The Human Condition*	解析汉娜·阿伦特《人的境况》	哲学
An Analysis of G.E.M. Anscombe's *Modern Moral Philosophy*	解析 G.E.M. 安斯康姆《现代道德哲学》	哲学
An Analysis of David Hume's *An Enquiry Concerning Human Understanding*	解析大卫·休谟《人类理解研究》	哲学

An Analysis of Søren Kierkegaard's *Fear and Trembling*	解析索伦·克尔凯郭尔《恐惧与战栗》	哲学
An Analysis of René Descartes's *Meditations on First Philosophy*	解析勒内·笛卡尔《第一哲学沉思录》	哲学
An Analysis of Friedrich Nietzsche's *On the Genealogy of Morality*	解析弗里德里希·尼采《论道德的谱系》	哲学
An Analysis of Gilbert Ryle's *The Concept of Mind*	解析吉尔伯特·赖尔《心的概念》	哲学
An Analysis of Thomas Kuhn's *The Structure of Scientific Revolutions*	解析托马斯·库恩《科学革命的结构》	哲学
An Analysis of John Stuart Mill's *Utilitarianism*	解析约翰·斯图亚特·穆勒《功利主义》	哲学
An Analysis of Aristotle's *Politics*	解析亚里士多德《政治学》	政治学
An Analysis of Niccolò Machiavelli's *The Prince*	解析尼科洛·马基雅维利《君主论》	政治学
An Analysis of Karl Marx's *Capital*	解析卡尔·马克思《资本论》	政治学
An Analysis of Benedict Anderson's *Imagined Communities*	解析本尼迪克特·安德森《想象的共同体》	政治学
An Analysis of Samuel P. Huntington's *The Clash of Civilizations and the Remaking of World Order*	解析塞缪尔·P.亨廷顿《文明的冲突与世界秩序重建》	政治学
An Analysis of Alexis de Tocqueville's *Democracy in America*	解析阿列克西·德·托克维尔《论美国的民主》	政治学
An Analysis of J. A. Hobson's *Imperialism: A Study*	解析约·阿·霍布森《帝国主义》	政治学
An Analysis of Thomas Paine's *Common Sense*	解析托马斯·潘恩《常识》	政治学
An Analysis of John Rawls's *A Theory of Justice*	解析约翰·罗尔斯《正义论》	政治学
An Analysis of Francis Fukuyama's *The End of History and the Last Man*	解析弗朗西斯·福山《历史的终结与最后的人》	政治学
An Analysis of John Locke's *Two Treatises of Government*	解析约翰·洛克《政府论》	政治学
An Analysis of Sun Tzu's *The Art of War*	解析孙武《孙子兵法》	政治学
An Analysis of Henry Kissinger's *World Order: Reflections on the Character of Nations and the Course of History*	解析亨利·基辛格《世界秩序》	政治学
An Analysis of Jean-Jacques Rousseau's *The Social Contract*	解析让-雅克·卢梭《社会契约论》	政治学

An Analysis of Odd Arne Westad's *The Global Cold War: Third World Interventions and the Making of Our Times*	解析文安立《全球冷战：美苏对第三世界的干涉与当代世界的形成》	政治学
An Analysis of Sigmund Freud's *The Interpretation of Dreams*	解析西格蒙德·弗洛伊德《梦的解析》	心理学
An Analysis of William James' *The Principles of Psychology*	解析威廉·詹姆斯《心理学原理》	心理学
An Analysis of Philip Zimbardo's *The Lucifer Effect*	解析菲利普·津巴多《路西法效应》	心理学
An Analysis of Leon Festinger's *A Theory of Cognitive Dissonance*	解析利昂·费斯汀格《认知失调论》	心理学
An Analysis of Richard H. Thaler & Cass R. Sunstein's *Nudge: Improving Decisions about Health, Wealth, and Happiness*	解析理查德·H.泰勒/卡斯·R.桑斯坦《助推：如何做出有关健康、财富和幸福的更优决策》	心理学
An Analysis of Gordon Allport's *The Nature of Prejudice*	解析高尔登·奥尔波特《偏见的本质》	心理学
An Analysis of Steven Pinker's *The Better Angels of Our Nature: Why Violence Has Declined*	解析斯蒂芬·平克《人性中的善良天使：暴力为什么会减少》	心理学
An Analysis of Stanley Milgram's *Obedience to Authority*	解析斯坦利·米尔格拉姆《对权威的服从》	心理学
An Analysis of Betty Friedan's *The Feminine Mystique*	解析贝蒂·弗里丹《女性的奥秘》	心理学
An Analysis of David Riesman's *The Lonely Crowd: A Study of the Changing American Character*	解析大卫·理斯曼《孤独的人群：美国人社会性格演变之研究》	社会学
An Analysis of Franz Boas's *Race, Language and Culture*	解析弗朗兹·博厄斯《种族、语言与文化》	社会学
An Analysis of Pierre Bourdieu's *Outline of a Theory of Practice*	解析皮埃尔·布尔迪厄《实践理论大纲》	社会学
An Analysis of Max Weber's *The Protestant Ethic and the Spirit of Capitalism*	解析马克斯·韦伯《新教伦理与资本主义精神》	社会学
An Analysis of Jane Jacobs's *The Death and Life of Great American Cities*	解析简·雅各布斯《美国大城市的死与生》	社会学
An Analysis of C. Wright Mills's *The Sociological Imagination*	解析C.赖特·米尔斯《社会学的想象力》	社会学
An Analysis of Robert E. Lucas Jr.'s *Why Doesn't Capital Flow from Rich to Poor Countries?*	解析小罗伯特·E.卢卡斯《为何资本不从富国流向穷国？》	社会学

An Analysis of Émile Durkheim's *On Suicide*	解析埃米尔·迪尔凯姆《自杀论》	社会学
An Analysis of Eric Hoffer's *The True Believer: Thoughts on the Nature of Mass Movements*	解析埃里克·霍弗《狂热分子：群众运动圣经》	社会学
An Analysis of Jared M. Diamond's *Collapse: How Societies Choose to Fail or Survive*	解析贾雷德·M.戴蒙德《大崩溃：社会如何选择兴亡》	社会学
An Analysis of Michel Foucault's *The History of Sexuality Vol. 1: The Will to Knowledge*	解析米歇尔·福柯《性史（第一卷）：求知意志》	社会学
An Analysis of Michel Foucault's *Discipline and Punish*	解析米歇尔·福柯《规训与惩罚》	社会学
An Analysis of Richard Dawkins's *The Selfish Gene*	解析理查德·道金斯《自私的基因》	社会学
An Analysis of Antonio Gramsci's *Prison Notebooks*	解析安东尼奥·葛兰西《狱中札记》	社会学
An Analysis of Augustine's *Confessions*	解析奥古斯丁《忏悔录》	神学
An Analysis of C. S. Lewis's *The Abolition of Man*	解析C.S.路易斯《人之废》	神学

图书在版编目（CIP）数据

解析马克斯·韦伯《新教伦理与资本主义精神》/ 塞巴斯蒂安·古兹曼，
詹姆斯·希尔（Sebasrián G. Guzmán with James Hill）著；杨静译. —上海：
上海外语教育出版社，2019
（世界思想宝库钥匙丛书）
ISBN 978-7-5446-5838-6

I.①解… Ⅱ.①塞… ②詹… ③杨… Ⅲ.①新教—研究—西方国家—汉、英
Ⅳ.①B976.3

中国版本图书馆CIP数据核字（2019）第076631号

This Chinese-English bilingual edition of *An Analysis of Max Weber's* The Protestant Ethic and
the Spirit of Capitalism is published by arrangement with Macat International Limited.
Licensed for sale throughout the world.

本书汉英双语版由Macat国际有限公司授权上海外语教育出版社有限公司出版。
供在全世界范围内发行、销售。

图字：09 – 2018 – 549

出版发行：**上海外语教育出版社**
（上海外国语大学内）　邮编：200083
电　　话：021-65425300（总机）
电子邮箱：bookinfo@sflep.com.cn
网　　址：http://www.sflep.com
责任编辑：李振荣

印　　刷：上海书刊印刷有限公司
开　　本：890×1240　1/32　印张6　字数123千字
版　　次：2019年8月第1版　2019年8月第1次印刷
印　　数：2 100册

书　　号：ISBN 978-7-5446-5838-6 / D
定　　价：30.00元

本版图书如有印装质量问题，可向本社调换
质量服务热线：4008-213-263　电子邮箱：editorial@sflep.com